Convention

Convention | A Philosophical Study

David Lewis

Harvard University Press
Cambridge, Massachusetts

For Steffi

Contents

Acknowledgements

I owe a pleasant debt to Willard Van Orman Quine for his encouragement and help throughout my effort to rehabilitate analyticity. I am grateful to my friends for their comments on earlier and later versions. Special thanks are due to George Boolos, Charles Chastain, David Kaplan, Ewart Lewis, Stephanie Lewis, Barbara Partee, Stephen Schiffer, Michael Slote, J. Howard Sobel, and the students in my seminar on philosophy of language at the University of California, Los Angeles, in the fall term of 1967. Warm thanks of another sort are due to the C'est Si Bon Pâtisserie, where most of this book was written, for their hospitality and their good coffee. I thank David Shwayder for permission to quote at length from his book *The Stratification of Behaviour*.

D. K. L.

Los Angeles
June 1968

Foreword

When I was a child I pictured our language as settled and passed down by a board of syndics, seated in grave convention along a table in the style of Rembrandt. The picture remained for a while undisturbed by the question what language the syndics might have used in their deliberations, or by dread of vicious regress.

I suppose this picture has been entertained by many, in uncritical childhood. Many mature thinkers, certainly, have called language conventional. Many have also in other connections been ready with appeals to agreements that were historically never enacted. The social contract, in Hobbes's theory of government, is the outstanding example. This case is logically more respectable than the language case; the notion that government began literally in a social contract involves no vicious regress.

Not, of course, that the proponents of the doctrine of social contract mean to be thus literally construed; they mean only that government is *as if* it had been thus established. But then this "as if" proposition raises the question, psychoanalytically speaking, of latent content: in just what ways is government like what an actual social contract might have given us? In the language case the question of latent content is even more urgent, and more perplexing, in that an original founding of language by overt convention is not merely unhistorical but unthinkable. What is convention when there can be no thought of convening?

Some philosophers have placed a heavy burden upon a purported distinction between truths that are *analytic,* these being true purely by linguistic convention, and the *synthetic* truths that say something substantial about reality. This is a characteristic and crucial case of appealing to convention where there can have been no thought of convening. For the philosophers in question count logical truth analytic; and here a circularity would arise if we were to take the conventions explicitly. The predicament is that in order to apply any explicit conventions that were general enough to afford all logical truth, we would already have to use logic in reasoning from the general conventions to the individual applications.

We have before us a study, both lucid and imaginative, both amusing and meticulous, in which Lewis undertakes to render the notion of convention independent of any fact or fiction of convening. He undertakes to isolate the distinguishing traits of conventionality, the latent content, without benefit of simile or make-believe. Very roughly, the keynote of conventionality is a certain indifference: the syllable "big" could have meant "small" for all we care, and the red light could have meant "go," and black ties could have been counted less formal than fancy ones. Such is the initial intuition; but the appropriate sense of indifference, or of "could have meant," needs a lot of refining. It gets it, thanks to Lewis' deft use, among other things, of the latter-day theory of games and decisions.

The problem of distinguishing between analytic and synthetic truths was apparently one motive of the study. In the end, Lewis concludes that the notion of convention is not the crux of this distinction. He does not for this reason find the analyticity notion unacceptable, however. He ends up rather where some began, resting the notion of analyticity on the notion of possible worlds. His contentment with this disposition of the analyticity problem makes one wonder, after all, how it culd have been much of a motive for his study of convention; but we may be thankful for whatever motives he had. For in the course of the book the reader comes to appreciate convention, not analyticity, as a key concept in the philosophy of language.

W. V. Quine

Harvard University
September 26, 1968

Convention

Introduction

It is the profession of philosophers to question platitudes that others accept without thinking twice. A dangerous profession, since philosophers are more easily discredited than platitudes, but a useful one. For when a good philosopher challenges a platitude, it usually turns out that the platitude was essentially right; but the philosopher has noticed trouble that one who did not think twice could not have met. In the end the challenge is answered and the platitude survives, more often than not. But the philosopher has done the adherents of the platitude a service: he has made them think twice.

It is a platitude that language is ruled by convention. Words might be used to mean almost anything; and we who use them have made them mean what they do because somehow, gradually and informally, we have come to an understanding that this is what we shall use them to mean. We could perfectly well use these words otherwise—or use different words, as men in foreign countries do. We might change our conventions if we like.

To say only this is not to say much. It is not to portray language in the image of a calculus, precise and rigid. It is not to uphold "correct" speech against colloquial, or vice versa. It is not to say that all the languages we can think of are equally good, or that every feature of a serviceable language might just as well have been different. It is not to say that necessary truths are created by convention: only that necessary truths, like geological truths, are conventionally stated in these words rather than in those. It is not to exalt the powers of convention as some "conventionalist" philosophers do,

I

but only to insist that it is there. The platitude that there are conventions of language is no dogma of any school of philosophy, but commands the immediate assent of any thoughtful person—unless he is a philosopher.

For this mere platitude has been challenged. W. V. Quine questioned it in 1936 and later repudiated it outright.[1] Morton White joined in the attack,[2] and together they have persuaded some to share their doubts, and reduced many more to silence. Quine and White argue that the supposed conventions of language cannot be very much like the central, well-understood cases of convention. Conventions are agreements—but did we ever agree with one another to abide by stipulated rules in our use of language? We did not. If our ancestors did, how should that concern us, who have forgotten? In any case, the conventions of language could not possibly have originated by agreement, since some of them would have been needed to provide the rudimentary language in which the first agreement was made. We cannot even say what our conventions are, except by long trial and error. Did we know them better when we first adopted them? We have no concept of convention which permits language to be conventional; we are inclined to call some features of language conventional, but we cannot say why. We may indulge this inclination—Quine himself does[3]—but we do not understand language any better for doing it. Conclusion: the conventions of language are a myth. The sober truth is that our use of language conforms to regularities—and that is all.

[1] "Truth by Convention," *Philosophical Essays for A. N. Whitehead,* ed. O. H. Lee (New York: Longmans, 1936); "Two Dogmas of Empiricism," *From a Logical Point of View: Nine Logico-Philosophical Essays,* 2nd ed. (Cambridge, Mass.: Harvard University Press, 1961), pp. 20–46; "Carnap and Logical Truth," *The Philosophy of Rudolf Carnap,* ed. P. A. Schilpp (LaSalle, Illinois: Open Court, 1963), pp. 385–406; *Word and Object* (Cambridge, Mass.: MIT Press, and New York: John Wiley, 1960).

[2] "The Analytic and the Synthetic: An Untenable Dualism," *John Dewey: Philosopher of Science and Freedom,* ed. Sidney Hook (New York: Dial, 1950), pp. 316–330; *Toward Reunion in Philosophy* (Cambridge, Mass.: Harvard University Press, 1956).

[3] At the end of "Carnap and Logical Truth" where he says: "The lore of our fathers . . . is a pale grey lore, black with fact and white with convention."

We may protest, desperately, that there must be *something* to our notion of conventions of language, even if we cannot say what. When we are exposed to the notion we *do* all manage to get the idea, and all of us go on more or less alike in distinguishing between features of language we call conventional and features of language we do not. So we must mean something. Conventionality must at least be that, we know not what, which evokes a distinctive response in anyone who has been through our kind of education.

But how much better it would be to know what we are talking about: to have an analysis of convention in its full generality, including tacit convention not created by agreement. This book is my attempt at an analysis. I hope it is an analysis of our common, established concept of convention, so that you will recognize that it explains what you must have had in mind when you said that language—like many other activities—is governed by conventions. But perhaps it is not, for perhaps not all of us do share any one clear general concept of convention. At least, insofar as *I* had a concept of convention before I thought twice, this is either it or its legitimate heir. And what I call convention is an important phenomenon under any name. Language is only one among many activities governed by conventions that we did not create by agreeing and that we cannot describe.

My theory of convention had its source in the theory of games of pure coordination—a neglected branch of the general theory of games of von Neumann and Morgenstern, very different in method and content from their successful and better known theory of games of pure conflict. Coordination games have been studied by Thomas C. Schelling,[4] and it is he who supplied me with the makings of an answer to Quine and White.

Yet, in the end, the theory of games is scaffolding. I can restate my analysis of convention without it. The result is a theory along the lines of Hume's, in his discussion of the origin of justice and property. Convention turns out to be

[4] *The Strategy of Conflict* (Cambridge, Mass.: Harvard University Press, 1960).

a general sense of common interest; which sense all the members of the society express to one another, and which induces them to regulate their conduct by certain rules. I observe that it will be to my interest [e.g.] to leave another in the possession of his goods, provided he will act in the same manner with regard to me. When this common sense of interest is mutually expressed and is known to both, it produces a suitable resolution and behavior. And this may properly enough be called a convention or agreement betwixt us, though without the interposition of a promise; since the actions of each of us have a reference to those of the other, and are performed upon the supposition that something is to be performed on the other part.[5]

[5] *A Treatise of Human Nature,* III.ii.2.

I | Coordination and Convention

1. Sample Coordination Problems

Use of language belongs to a class of situations with a conspicuous common character: situations I shall call *coordination problems*. I postpone a definition until we have seen a few examples. We begin with situations that might arise between two people—call them "you" and "I."

(1) Suppose you and I both want to meet each other. We will meet if and only if we go to the same place. It matters little to either of us where (within limits) he goes if he meets the other there; and it matters little to either of us where he goes if he fails to meet the other there. We must each choose where to go. The best place for me to go is the place where you will go, so I try to figure out where you will go and to go there myself. You do the same. Each chooses according to his expectation of the other's choice. If either succeeds, so does the other; the outcome is one we both desired.

(2) Suppose you and I are talking on the telephone and we are unexpectedly cut off after three minutes. We both want the connection restored immediately, which it will be if and only if one of us calls back while the other waits. It matters little to either of us whether he is the one to call back or the one to wait. We must each choose whether to call back, each according to his expectation of the other's choice, in order to call back if and only if the other waits.

(3) An example from Hume's *Treatise of Human Nature:* Suppose you and I are rowing a boat together. If we row in rhythm, the boat goes smoothly forward; otherwise the boat goes slowly and erratically,

we waste effort, and we risk hitting things. We are always choosing whether to row faster or slower; it matters little to either of us at what rate we row, provided we row in rhythm. So each is constantly adjusting his rate to match the rate he expects the other to maintain.

Now we turn to situations among more than two people.

(4) Suppose several of us are driving on the same winding two-lane roads. It matters little to anyone whether he drives in the left or the right lane, provided the others do likewise. But if some drive in the left lane and some in the right, everyone is in danger of collision. So each must choose whether to drive in the left lane or in the right, according to his expectations about the others: to drive in the left lane if most or all of the others do, to drive in the right lane if most or all of the others do (and to drive where he pleases if the others are more or less equally divided).

(5) Suppose we are campers who have gone looking for firewood. It matters little to anyone in which direction he goes, but if any two go in the same direction they are likely to cover the same ground so that the one who gets there later finds no wood. Each must choose a direction to go according to his expectations about the others: one different from anyone else's.

(6) Suppose several of us have been invited to a party. It matters little to anyone how he dresses. But he would be embarrassed if the others dressed alike and he dressed differently, since he knows that some discreditable explanation for that difference can be produced by whoever is so inclined. So each must dress according to his expectations about the way the others will dress: in a tuxedo if the others will wear tuxedos, in a clown suit if the others will wear clown suits (and in what he pleases if the others will dress in diverse ways).

(7) Suppose we are contented oligopolists. As the price of our raw material varies, we must each set new prices. It is to no one's advantage to set his prices higher than the others set theirs, since if he does he tends to lose his share of the market. Nor is it to anyone's advantage to set his prices lower than the others set theirs, since if he does he menaces his competitors and incurs their retaliation. So each must

set his prices within the range of prices he expects the others to set.

(8) An example from Rousseau's *Discours sur l'inégalité:* Suppose we are in a wilderness without food. Separately we can catch rabbits and eat badly. Together we can catch stags and eat well. But if even one of us deserts the stag hunt to catch a rabbit, the stag will get away; so the other stag hunters will not eat unless they desert too. Each must choose whether to stay with the stag hunt or desert according to his expectations about the others, staying if and only if no one else will desert.

(9) Suppose we take it to be in our common interest that some scarce good, say grazing land, should be divided up somehow so that each of us can count on having the exclusive use of one portion. (Suppose nobody ever thinks it would be in his interest to help himself to someone else's portion. The struggle, the harm to his neighbor, the bad example, the general loss of confidence, invariably seem to outweigh any gain.) It matters little to anyone who uses which portion, so long as people never try to use the same portion and no portion ever goes to waste. Each must choose which portion to use according to his expectations about the portions others will use and the portion they will leave for him.

(10) Suppose we are tradesmen. It matters little to any of us what commodities he takes in exchange for goods (other than commodities he himself can use). But if he takes what others refuse he is stuck with something useless, and if he refuses what others take he needlessly inconveniences his customers and himself. Each must choose what he will take according to his expectations about what he can spend—that is, about what the others will take: gold and silver if he can spend gold and silver, U.S. notes if he can spend U.S. notes, Canadian pennies if he can spend Canadian pennies, wampum if he can spend wampum, goats if he can spend goats, whatever may come along if he can spend whatever may come along, nothing if he can spend nothing.

(11) Suppose that with practice we could adopt any language in some wide range. It matters comparatively little to anyone (in the

long run) what language he adopts, so long as he and those around him adopt the same language and can communicate easily. Each must choose what language to adopt according to his expectations about his neighbors' language: English among English speakers, Welsh among Welsh speakers, Esperanto among Esperanto speakers, and so on.

2. Analysis of Coordination Problems

With these examples, let us see how to describe the common character of coordination problems.

Two or more agents must each choose one of several alternative actions. Often all the agents have the same set of alternative actions, but that is not necessary. The outcomes the agents want to produce or prevent are determined jointly by the actions of all the agents. So the outcome of any action an agent might choose depends on the actions of the other agents. That is why—as we have seen in every example—each must choose what to do according to his expectations about what the others will do.

Some combinations of the agents' chosen actions are *equilibria:* combinations in which each agent has done as well as he can given the actions of the other agents. In an equilibrium combination, no one agent could have produced an outcome more to his liking by acting differently, unless some of the others' actions also had been different. No one regrets his choice after he learns how the others chose. No one has lost through lack of foreknowledge.

This is not to say that an equilibrium combination must produce an outcome that is best for even one of the agents (though if there is a combination that is best for everyone, that combination must be an equilibrium). In an equilibrium, it is entirely possible that some or all of the agents would have been better off if some or all had acted differently. What is not possible is that any one of the agents would have been better off if he alone had acted differently and all the rest had acted just as they did.

We can illustrate equilibria by drawing *payoff matrices* for coordination problems between two agents. Call the agents *Row-chooser* and *Column-chooser.* We represent Row-chooser's alternative actions by labeled rows of the matrix, and Column-chooser's by labeled columns. The squares then represent combinations of the agents' actions and the expected outcomes thereof. Squares are labeled with two *payoffs,* numbers somehow measuring the desirability of the expected outcome for Row-chooser and Column-chooser.[1] Row-chooser's payoff is at the lower left, Column-chooser's at the upper right.

Thus the matrix of Figure 1 might represent a simple version of example (1), where *R1*, *R2*, and *R3* are Row-chooser's actions of

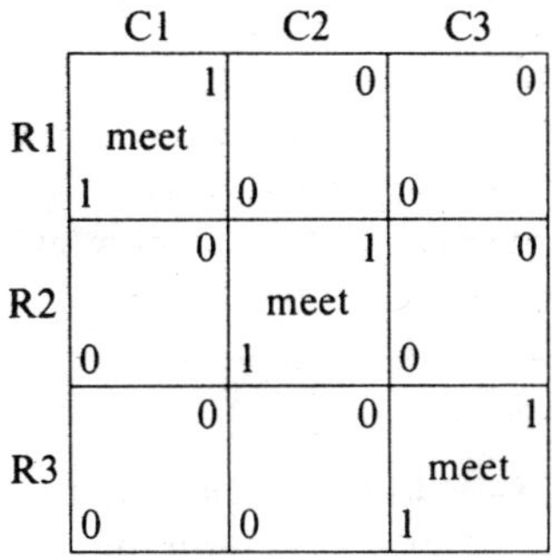

	C1	C2	C3
R1	1 meet 1	0 0	0 0
R2	0 0	1 meet 1	0 0
R3	0 0	0 0	1 meet 1

Figure 1

going places *P1*, *P2*, and *P3* respectively, and *C1*, *C2*, and *C3* are Column-chooser's actions of going to places *P1*, *P2*, and *P3* respectively. The equilibria are the three combinations in which Row-

[1] My account will demand no great sophistication about these numerical measures of desirability. If a foundation is required, it could be provided by decision theory as developed, for instance, by Richard Jeffrey in *The Logic of Decision* (New York: McGraw-Hill, 1965). I take it that decision theory applies in some approximate way to ordinary rational agents with imperfectly coherent preferences; our payoffs need never be more than rough indications of strength of preference.

chooser and Column-chooser go to the same place and meet there: $\langle R1, C1 \rangle$, $\langle R2, C2 \rangle$, and $\langle R3, C3 \rangle$. For instance, $\langle R2, C2 \rangle$ is an equilibrium by definition because Row-chooser prefers it to $\langle R1, C2 \rangle$ or $\langle R3, C2 \rangle$, and Column-chooser prefers it to $\langle R2, C1 \rangle$ or $\langle R2, C3 \rangle$. Both are indifferent between the three equilibria.

But suppose we change the example so that Row-chooser and Column-chooser care where they go, though not nearly so much as they care whether they meet. The new payoff matrix might be as shown in Figure 2. The equilibria remain the same: $\langle R1, C1 \rangle$,

	C1	C2	C3
R1	1.5 meet 1.5	.2 .5	0 .5
R2	.5 .2	1.2 meet 1.2	0 .2
R3	.5 0	.2 0	1 meet 1

Figure 2

$\langle R2, C2 \rangle$, and $\langle R3, C3 \rangle$. But Row-chooser and Column-chooser are no longer indifferent between the equilibria. $\langle R1, C1 \rangle$ is the best possible outcome for both; $\langle R3, C3 \rangle$ is the worst equilibrium outcome for both, though both prefer it to the nonequilibrium outcomes. Or if the payoff matrix were as shown in Figure 3, then $\langle R1, C1 \rangle$ would be Row-chooser's best outcome and Column-chooser's worst equilibrium outcome; $\langle R3, C3 \rangle$ would be Column-chooser's best outcome and Row-chooser's worst equilibrium outcome. No outcome would be best for both.

There seems to be a difference between equilibrium combinations in which every agent does the same action and equilibrium combinations in which agents do different actions. This difference is spurious, however. We say that the agents do the same action if they do actions

	C1	C2	C3
R1	1 meet 1.5	.2 .5	.5 .5
R2	0 .2	1.2 meet 1.2	.5 .2
R3	0 0	.2 0	1.5 meet 1

Figure 3

of the same kind, particular actions falling under a common description. But actions can be described in any number of ways, of which none has any compelling claim to primacy. For *any* combination of actions, and *a fortiori* for any equilibrium combination of actions, there is *some* way of describing the agents' alternative actions so that exactly those alternative actions in the given combination fall under a common description. Any combination, equilibrium or not, is a combination of actions of *a* same kind (a kind that excludes all the agents' alternative actions). Whether it can be called a combination in which every agent does the same action depends merely on the naturalness of that classification.

Consider example (2). If we have in mind these action-descriptions,

> *R1* or *C1*: calling back
> *R2* or *C2*: not calling back

we draw the payoff matrix shown in Figure 4 and think of the case as one in which the equilibria ⟨*R1, C2*⟩ and ⟨*R2, C1*⟩ are combinations in which the agents do different actions. But if we have in mind these action-descriptions,

> *R1′* or *C1′*: calling back if and only if one is the original caller
> *R2′* or *C2′*: calling back if and only if one is not the original caller

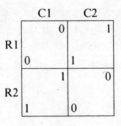

Figure 4

we draw the payoff matrix shown in Figure 5 and think of the case as one in which the equilibria $\langle R1', C1' \rangle$ and $\langle R2', C2' \rangle$ are combi-

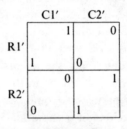

Figure 5

nations in which the agents do the same action. But what makes the first pair of action-descriptions more natural than the second? And so what if it is?

We might say that coordination problems are situations in which several agents try to achieve uniformity of action by each doing whatever the others will do. But this is a dangerous thing to say, since it is true of a coordination problem only under suitable descriptions of actions, and sometimes the descriptions that make it true would strike us as contrived—so, for instance, in examples (2), (5), (9), and perhaps (4). What is important about the uniform combinations we are interested in is not that they are—under some description—uniform, but that they are equilibria.

Of course this is not to say that coordination problems are distinguished by the presence of equilibria. Indeed the bulk of the mathematical theory of games is precisely the theory of equilibrium combinations (known also as *saddle points* or *solutions*) in situations of the opposite kind: pure conflict of interest between two agents, as in Figure 6.

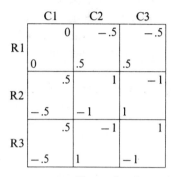

Figure 6

In general, pure conflict can be represented by a payoff matrix in which the agents' payoffs (perhaps after suitable linear rescaling) sum to zero in every square.[2] This is to say that one agent's losses are the others' gains, and vice versa. Yet there are equilibria in pure conflict. In the example shown, $\langle R1, C1 \rangle$ is an equilibrium: Row-chooser prefers it to $\langle R2, C1 \rangle$ or $\langle R3, C1 \rangle$, and Column-chooser prefers it to $\langle R1, C2 \rangle$ or $\langle R1, C3 \rangle$.

Schelling argues for a "reorientation of game theory" in which games—problems of interdependent decision—are taken to range over a spectrum with games of pure conflict and games of pure coordination as opposite limits.[3] *Games of pure conflict,* in which the

[2] There is no point in changing the definition to let the sum be a constant other than zero. By allowing rescaling, we already have full generality. Without rescaling, we would not reach full generality just by allowing nonzero constant sums. And by allowing linear rescaling, we make clear why—despite appearance—our definitions do not depend on any problematic interpersonal comparison of desirabilities.

[3] *Strategy of Conflict,* pp. 83–118, 291–303.

agents' interests are perfectly opposed, can be defined as we have just seen. *Games of pure coordination,* in which the agents' interests coincide perfectly, are games in which the agents' payoffs (perhaps after suitable linear rescaling) are equal in every square. Other games are mixtures in varying proportions of conflict and coordination, of opposition and coincidence of interests.

My coordination problems such as (1)–(11) are among the situations at or near the pure coordination end of Schelling's spectrum. I do not want to require perfect coincidence of interests. For instance, I allowed imperfect coincidence of interests in those versions of example (1) in which Row-chooser and Column-chooser care somewhat where they go, though much less than they care whether they meet. We recall the payoff matrices of Figures 2 and 3 (pp. 10–11). In several squares, the payoffs are not quite equal. No linear rescaling of either matrix could make them equal in every square at once.

I want, however, to confine my attention to situations in which coincidence of interest predominates: that is, in which the differences between different agents' payoffs in any one square (perhaps after suitable linear rescaling) are small compared to some of the differences between payoffs in different squares. So they are in the matrices of Figures 2 and 3; the largest difference within one square is .5, whereas the largest difference between payoffs in different squares is 1.5.

An equilibrium, we recall, is a combination in which no one would have been better off had he alone acted otherwise. Let me define a *coordination equilibrium* as a combination in which no one would have been better off had *any one* agent alone acted otherwise, either himself or someone else. Coordination equilibria are equilibria, by the definitions. Equilibria in games of pure coordination are always coordination equilibria, since the agents' interests coincide perfectly. Any game of pure coordination has at least one coordination equilibrium, since it has at least one outcome that is best for all. But coordination equilibria are by no means confined to games of pure coordination. They are common in situations with mixed opposition and coincidence of interests. They can occur even in games of pure conflict: $\langle R1, C1 \rangle$ in Figure 7 is a coordination equilibrium.

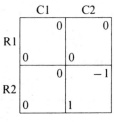

Figure 7

Most versions of our sample coordination problems are not games of pure coordination; but they all have coordination equilibria. We have noticed that the versions of the meeting-place problem shown in Figures 2 and 3 are not games of pure coordination; but their equilibria—$\langle R1, C1 \rangle$, $\langle R2, C2 \rangle$, and $\langle R3, C3 \rangle$ in both versions—are coordination equilibria.

This is not to say that *all* the equilibria in a coordination problem must be coordination equilibria. Take still another version of example (1). Suppose there is a fourth place, *P4*. Row-chooser and Column-chooser both like to go to *P4* alone, but a meeting at *P4* would detract from their enjoyment of going to *P4* and *P4* would be of little use as a meeting place. So we have the matrix shown in Figure 8, with the usual coordination equilibria $\langle R1, C1 \rangle$, $\langle R2, C2 \rangle$, $\langle R3, C3 \rangle$ and a new *non*coordination equilibrium $\langle R4, C4 \rangle$. It is an equilibrium because Row-chooser prefers it to $\langle R1, C4 \rangle$, $\langle R2, C4 \rangle$, or $\langle R3, C4 \rangle$, and Column-chooser prefers it to $\langle R4, C1 \rangle$, $\langle R4, C2 \rangle$, or $\langle R4, C3 \rangle$. It is not a coordination equilibrium because not all—in fact, none—of these preferences are shared by Row-chooser and Column-chooser. Yet this version of (1) does not seem significantly different from the others. The situation still has that distinctive character which I introduced by means of my eleven examples. So let us tolerate noncoordination equilibria in coordination problems.

	C1	C2	C3	C4
R1	1 / meet / 1	0 / 0	0 / 0	.5 / 0
R2	0 / 0	1 / meet / 1	0 / 0	.5 / 0
R3	0 / 0	0 / 0	1 / meet / 1	.5 / 0
R4	0 / .5	0 / .5	0 / .5	.2 / meet / .2

Figure 8

All my sample coordination problems have two or more different coordination equilibria. This multiplicity is important to the distinctive character of coordination problems and ought to be included in their definition. If there is no considerable conflict of interest, the task of reaching a unique coordination equilibrium is more or less trivial. It will be reached if the nature of the situation is clear enough so that everybody makes the best choice given his expectations, everybody expects everybody else to make the best choice given his expectations, and so on. These conditions do not ensure coordination if there are multiple coordination equilibria, as we shall see.

Many of the situations with unique coordination equilibria are still

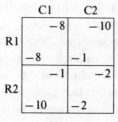

Figure 9

more trivial (and more deserving of exclusion). For instance, any situation in which all the agents have [*strictly*] *dominant* choices—actions they prefer no matter what the others do—can have only one equilibrium (and *a fortiori* only one coordination equilibrium), namely, the combination of dominant choices. A combination of dominant choices must be an equilibrium; but it might not be a coordination equilibrium, as in the well-known Prisoner's Dilemma, shown in Figure 9, in which $R1$ and $C1$ (treacherous confession, in the usual story) are dominant and their combination $\langle R1, C1 \rangle$ is a noncoordination equilibrium.

We might guess that there is dominance in *any* game of pure coordination with a unique equilibrium: that all, or at least some, agents have dominant, or at least dominated, choices. (A [*strictly*] *dominated* choice is one such that, no matter how the others choose, you could have made some other choice that would have been better. If one choice is dominant, another must be dominated; but not vice versa, since *which* other choice would have been better for you may depend on how the others chose.) There is this much truth in the guess: in any finite two-person game of pure coordination with a unique equilibrium, at least one action of one of the agents is dominated. Proof:

Let $P(\langle Rj, Ck \rangle)$ represent the payoff at the combination $\langle Rj, Ck \rangle$, equal for Row-chooser and Column-chooser.

Take a suitable game with m rows and n columns. Assume without loss of generality that its rows and columns are so arranged that for any combination $\langle Ri, Ci \rangle$ on the diagonal and any combination $\langle Rj, Ck \rangle$ such that $j \geq i$ and $k \geq i$, $P(\langle Rj, Ck \rangle) \leq P(\langle Ri, Ci \rangle)$. In particular, $\langle R1, C1 \rangle$ must be the unique equilibrium, and $P(\langle R1, C1 \rangle)$ must exceed every other payoff in the game.

If $\langle R1, C1 \rangle$ is the only diagonal combination that is either a row-maximum or a column-maximum, then Rm (if $m \geq n$) or Cn (if $n \geq m$) must be dominated.

Otherwise let $\langle Ra, Ca \rangle$, $a \neq 1$, be the rightmost diagonal combination which is either a row-maximum or a column-maximum. It is not both, since it is not an equilibrium. Suppose without loss of generality that it is a row-maximum.

Unless Ra is strictly dominated, there is a column-maximum on Ra; let $\langle Ra, Cb \rangle$ be the rightmost one. $\langle Ra, Cb \rangle$ is not a row-maximum since it is not an equilibrium, so $P(\langle Ra, Ca \rangle) > P(\langle Ra, Cb \rangle)$.

Unless Cb is strictly dominated, there is a row-maximum on Cb; let $\langle Ra', Cb \rangle$ be the lowest one. Since $\langle Ra, Cb \rangle$ is a column-maximum, $P(\langle Ra, Cb \rangle) \geq P(\langle Ra', Cb \rangle)$, so $P(\langle Ra, Ca \rangle) > P(\langle Ra', Cb \rangle)$.

Unless Ra' is strictly dominated there is a column-maximum on Ra'; let $\langle Ra', Cb' \rangle$ be the rightmost one; $P(\langle Ra, Ca \rangle) > P(\langle Ra', Cb' \rangle)$.

Unless Cb' is strictly dominated, there is a row-maximum on Cb'; let $\langle Ra'', Cb' \rangle$ be the lowest one; $P(\langle Ra, Ca \rangle) > P(\langle Ra'', Cb' \rangle)$.

Unless Ra'' is strictly dominated, there is a column-maximum on Ra''; let $\langle Ra'', Cb'' \rangle$ be the rightmost one; $P(\langle Ra, Ca \rangle) > P(\langle Ra'', Cb'' \rangle)$. And so on.

If $\langle Rj, Ci \rangle$ is a column-maximum and $P(\langle Ra, Ca \rangle) > P(\langle Rj, Ci \rangle)$, then $\langle Rj, Ci \rangle$ is above the diagonal. For otherwise $j \geq i$, so $P(\langle Rj, Ci \rangle) \leq P(\langle Ri, Ci \rangle)$. And since $\langle Rj, Ci \rangle$ is a column-maximum, $P(\langle Rj, Ci \rangle) = P(\langle Ri, Ci \rangle)$. Then $\langle Ri, Ci \rangle$ is also a column-maximum, and it is to the right of $\langle Ra, Ca \rangle$ since $P(\langle Ra, Ca \rangle) > P(\langle Ri, Ci \rangle)$. But that is contrary to our choice of $\langle Ra, Ca \rangle$.

In particular: $\langle Ra, Cb \rangle$, $\langle Ra', Cb' \rangle$, $\langle Ra'', Cb'' \rangle$, etc. are above the diagonal.

By a parallel argument, if $\langle Rj, Ci \rangle$ is a row-maximum and $P(\langle Ra, Ca \rangle) > P(\langle Rj, Ci \rangle)$, then $\langle Rj, Ci \rangle$ is below the diagonal. In particular: $\langle Ra', Cb \rangle$, $\langle Ra'', Cb' \rangle$, etc. are below the diagonal.

Therefore the sequence of combinations we were constructing

moves back and forth across the diagonal, as shown in Figure 10, so that $a < a' < a''$. . . and $b < b' < b''$. . . . Since the game is finite, these sequences terminate, which can happen only if one of Ra, Cb, Ra', Cb', Ra'', Cb'' etc. is strictly dominated.

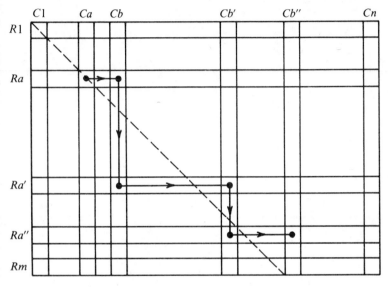

Figure 10

The deletion of a dominated action in a finite two-person game of pure coordination with a unique equilibrium leaves a new game, which is itself a finite two-person game of pure coordination with a unique equilibrium. So the deletion can be repeated. By successive deletions of dominated actions, the game is transformed into a situation that is patently trivial because Row-chooser and Column-chooser each have only one available action. The outcome is determined by the fact that everybody ignores dominated actions, everybody expects everybody else to ignore dominated actions, and so on.

The result just proved cannot, unfortunately, be strengthened in any of the ways one might hope. It does not carry over to infinite two-person games; Figure 11 is a counterexample. It does not carry over to finite three-person games; Figure 12 is a counterexample.

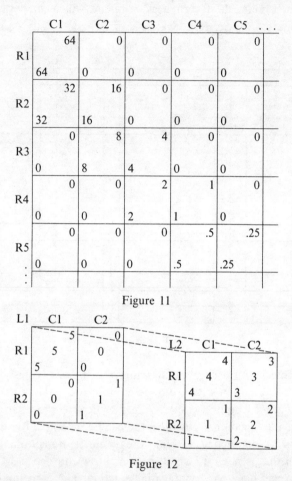

Figure 11

Figure 12

(Call the third agent's choices *levels L1* and *L2*; write his payoffs in the centers of the squares.) It cannot be strengthened for the finite two-person case; Figure 13 is an example with no dominant action and only a single dominated action (and that one is dominated only

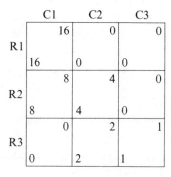

Figure 13

by all the alternatives together). Therefore we cannot say that dom-inance is responsible for all cases of unique equilibria in games of pure coordination.

To exclude trivial cases, a coordination problem must have more than one coordination equilibrium. But that requirement is not quite strong enough. Figure 14 shows two matrices in which, sure enough,

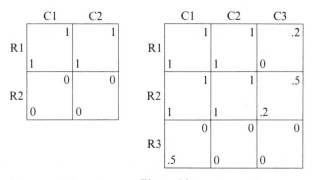

Figure 14

there are multiple coordination equilibria (two on the left, four on the right). Yet there is still no need for either agent to base his choice on his expectation about the other's choice. There is no need for them to try for the same equilibrium—no need for coordination—since if they try for different equilibria, some equilbrium will nevertheless be reached. These cases exhibit another kind of triviality, akin to the triviality of a case with a unique coordination equilibrium.

A combination is an equilibrium if each agent likes it *at least as well as* any other combination he could have reached, given the others' choices. Let us call it a *proper* equilibrium if each agent likes it *better than* any other combination he could have reached, given the others' choices. In a two-person matrix, for instance, a proper equilibrium is preferred by Row-chooser to all other combinations in its column, and by Column-chooser to all other combinations in its row. In the matrices in Figure 14, there are multiple coordination equilibria, but all of them are improper.

There is no need to stipulate that all equilibria in a coordination problem must be proper; it seems that the matrix in Figure 15 ought to be counted as essentially similar to our clear examples of coordina-

	C1	C2	C3
R1	2 / 2	0 / 0	0 / 0
R2	0 / 0	2 / 2	0 / 0
R3	0 / 0	1 / 1	1 / 1

Figure 15

tion problems, despite the impropriety of its equilibrium ⟨*R3, C3*⟩. The two proper coordination equilibria—⟨*R1, C1*⟩ and ⟨*R2, C2*⟩—are sufficient to keep the problem nontrivial. I stipulate instead that a coordination problem must contain at least two proper coordination equilibria.

This is only one—the strongest—of several defensible restrictions. We might prefer a weaker restriction that would not rule out matrices like those in Figure 16. But a satisfactory restriction would be com-

	C1	C2	C3
R1	1 / 1	0 / 0	0 / 0
R2	0 / 0	1 / 1	1 / 1
R3	0 / 0	1 / 1	1 / 1

	C1	C2	C3	C4
R1	1 / 1	1 / 1	0 / 0	0 / 0
R2	1 / 1	1 / 1	0 / 0	0 / 0
R3	0 / 0	0 / 0	1 / 1	1 / 1
R4	0 / 0	0 / 0	1 / 1	1 / 1

Figure 16

plicated and would entail too many qualifications later. And situations like those of Figure 16 can be rescued even under the strong restriction we have adopted. Let $R2'$ be the disjunction of $R2$ and $R3$, and $C2'$ the disjunction of $C2$ and $C3$ in the left-hand matrix. Then the same situation can be represented by the new matrix in Figure 17, which does have two proper coordination equilibria. The

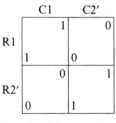

Figure 17

right-hand matrix can be consolidated in a similar way. But matrices like the one in Figure 18, which are ruled out by the strong restriction, and ought to be ruled out, cannot be rescued by any such consolidation.

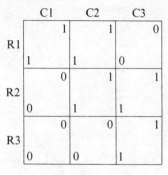

Figure 18

To sum up: Coordination problems—situations that resemble my eleven examples in the important respects in which they resemble one another[4]—are situations of interdependent decision by two or more agents in which coincidence of interest predominates and in which there are two or more proper coordination equilibria. We could also say—though less informatively than one might think—that they are situations in which, relative to *some* classification of actions, the agents have a common interest in all doing the same one of several alternative actions.

3. Solving Coordination Problems

Agents confronted by a coordination problem may or may not succeed in each acting so that they reach one of the possible coordination equilibria. They might succeed just by luck, although some of them choose without regard to the others' expected actions (doing so perhaps because they cannot guess what the others will do, perhaps because the chance of coordination seems so small as to be negligible).

[4] See Michael Slote, "The Theory of Important Criteria," *Journal of Philosophy*, 63 (1966), pp. 211–224. Slote shows that we commonly introduce a class by means of examples and take the defining features of the class to be those distinctive features of our examples which seem important for an understanding of their character. That is what I take myself to be doing here and elsewhere.

But they are more likely to succeed—if they do—through the agency of a system of suitably concordant mutual expectations. Thus in example (1) I may go to a certain place because I expect you to go there, while you go there because you expect me to; in example (2) I may call back because I expect you not to, while you do not because you expect me to; in example (4) each of us may drive on the right because he expects the rest to do so; and so on. In general, each may do his part of one of the possible coordination equilibria because he expects the others to do theirs, thereby reaching that equilibrium.

If an agent were completely confident in his expectation that the others would do their parts of a certain proper coordination equilibrium, he would have a decisive reason to do his own part. But if—as in any real case—his confidence is less than complete, he must balance his preference for doing his part if the others do theirs against his preferences for acting otherwise if they do not. He has a decisive reason to do his own part if he is *sufficiently* confident in his expectation that the others will do theirs. The degree of confidence which is sufficient depends on all his payoffs and sometimes on the comparative probabilities he assigns to the different *ways* the others might not all do their parts, in case not all of them do. For instance, in the coordination problem shown in Figure 19, Row-chooser should

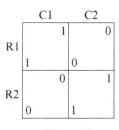

Figure 19

do his part of the coordination equilibrium ⟨*R1, C1*⟩ by choosing *R1* if he has more than .5 confidence that Column-chooser will do his part by choosing *C1*. But in the coordination problems shown in Figure 20, Row-chooser should choose R1 only if he has more

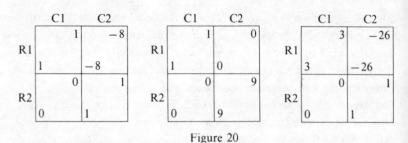

Figure 20

than .9 confidence that Column-chooser will choose *C1*. If he has, say, .8 confidence that Column-chooser will choose *C1*, he would do better to choose *R2*, sacrificing his chance to achieve coordination at ⟨*R1*, *C1*⟩ in order to hedge against the possibility that his expectation was wrong. And in the coordination problem shown in Figure 21, Row-chooser might be sure that if Column-chooser fails to do

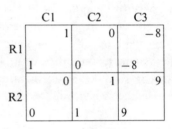

Figure 21

his part of ⟨*R1*, *C1*⟩, at least he will choose *C2*, not *C3*; if so, Row-chooser should choose *R1* if he has more than .5 confidence that Column-chooser will choose *C1*. Or Row-chooser might think that if Column-chooser fails to choose *R1*, he is just as likely to choose *C3* as to choose *C2*; if so, Row-chooser should choose *R1* only if he has more than .9 confidence that Column-chooser will choose *C1*. Or Row-chooser might be sure that if Column-chooser does not choose *C1*, he will choose *C3* instead; if so, Row-chooser's minimum sufficient degree of confidence is about .95. The strength of concordant expectation needed to produce coordination at a certain equilibrium is a measure of the difficulty of achieving coordination there, since however the concordant expectations are produced, weaker expectations will be produced more easily than stronger ones. (We can imagine cases in which so much mutual confidence is required to achieve coordination at an equilibrium that success is impossible. Imagine that a millionaire offers to distribute his fortune equally among a thousand men if each sends him $10; if even one does not, the millionaire will keep whatever he is sent. I take it that no matter what the thousand do to increase their mutual confidence, it is a practical certainty that the millionaire will not have to pay up. So if I am one of the thousand, I will keep my $10.)

We may achieve coordination by acting on our concordant expectations about each other's actions. And we may acquire those expectations, or correct or corroborate whatever expectations we already have, by putting ourselves in the other fellow's shoes, to the best of our ability. If I know what you believe about the matters of fact that determine the likely effects of your alternative actions, and if I know your preferences among possible outcomes and I know that you possess a modicum of practical rationality, then I can replicate your practical reasoning to figure out what you will probably do, so that I can act appropriately.

In the case of a coordination problem, or any other problem of interdependent decision, one of the matters of fact that goes into determining the likely effects of your alternative actions is my own action. In order to figure out what you will do by replicating your practical reasoning, I need to figure out what *you* expect *me* to do.

I know that, just as I am trying to figure out what you will do by replicating your reasoning, so you may be trying to figure out what I will do by replicating my reasoning. This, like anything else you might do to figure out what I will do, is itself part of your reasoning. So to replicate your reasoning, I may have to replicate your attempt to replicate my reasoning

This is not the end. I may reasonably expect *you* to realize that, unless I already know what you expect me to do, I may have to try to replicate your attempt to replicate my reasoning. So I may expect you to try to replicate my attempt to replicate your attempt to replicate my reasoning. So my own reasoning may have to include an attempt to replicate your attempt to replicate my attempt to replicate your attempt to replicate my reasoning. And so on.

Before things get out of hand, it will prove useful to introduce the concept of *higher-order expectations*, defined by recursion thus:

> A first-order expectation about something is an ordinary expectation about it.
>
> An $(n + 1)$th-order expectation about something $(n \geq 1)$ is an ordinary expectation about someone else's nth-order expectation about it.

For instance, if I expect you to expect that it will thunder, then I have a second-order expectation that it will thunder.

Whenever I replicate a piece of your practical reasoning, my second-order expectations about matters of fact, together with my first-order expectations about your preferences and your rationality, justify me in forming a first-order expectation about your action. In the case of problems of interdependent decision—for instance, coordination problems—some of the requisite second-order expectations must be about my own action.

Consider our first sample coordination problem: a situation in which you and I want to meet by going to the same place. Suppose that after deliberation I decide to come to a certain place. The fundamental practical reasoning which leads me to that choice is shown in Figure 22. (In all diagrams of this kind, heavy arrows represent implications; light arrows represent causal connections between the mental states or actions of a rational agent.) And if my premise for this reasoning—my expectation that you will go there—was obtained by replicating your reasoning, my replication is shown in Figure 23. And if my premise for this replication—my expectation that you will expect me to go there—was obtained by replicating your replication of my reasoning, my replication of your replication is shown in Figure 24. And so on. The whole of my reasoning (simplified by disregarding the rationality premises) may be represented as in

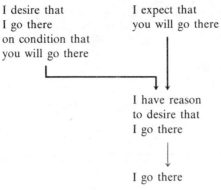

Figure 22

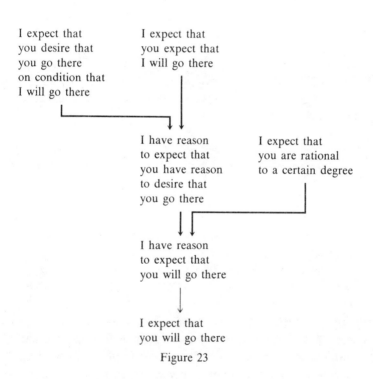

Figure 23

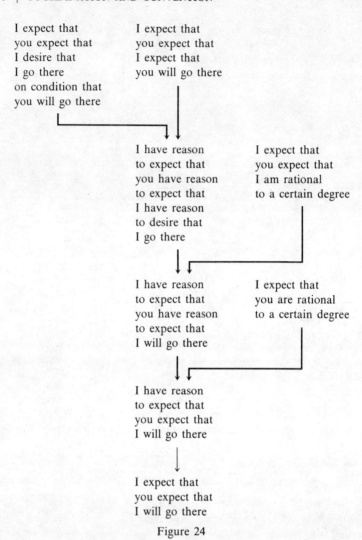

Figure 24

Figure 25 for whatever finite number of stages it may take for me to use whatever higher-order expectations may be available to me regarding our actions and our conditional preferences. Replications are nested to some finite depth: my reasoning (outer boundary) con-

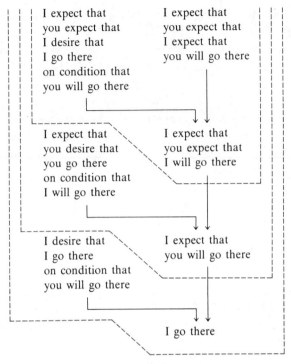

I expect that
you expect that
I desire that
I go there
on condition that
you will go there

I expect that
you expect that
I expect that
you will go there

I expect that
you desire that
you go there
on condition that
I will go there

I expect that
you expect that
I will go there

I desire that
I go there
on condition that
you will go there

I expect that
you will go there

I go there

Figure 25

tains a replication of yours (next boundary), which contains a replication of your replication of mine (next boundary), and so on.

So if I somehow happen to have an nth-order expectation about action in this two-person coordination problem, I may work outward through the nested replications to lower- and lower-order expectations about action. Provided I go on long enough, and provided all the needed higher-order expectations about preferences and rationality are available, I eventually come out with a first-order expectation about your action—which is what I need in order to know how I should act.

Clearly a similar process of replication is possible in coordination problems among more than two agents. In general, my higher-order expectations about something are my expectations about x_1's expectations about x_2's expectations . . . about it. (The sequence x_1, x_2 . . . may repeat, but x_1 cannot be myself and no one can occur twice in immediate succession.) So when m agents are involved, I can have as many as $(m - 1)^n$ different nth-order expectations about anything, corresponding to the $(m - 1)^n$ different admissible sequences of length n. Replication in general is ramified: it is built from stages in which $m - 1$ of my various $(n + 1)$th-order expectations about action, plus ancillary premises, yield one of my nth-order expectations about action. I suppressed the ramification by setting $m = 2$, but the general case is the same in principle.

Note that replication is *not* an interaction back and forth between people. It is a process in which *one* person works out the consequences of his beliefs about the world—a world he believes to include other people who are working out the consequences of their beliefs, including their belief in other people who . . . By our interaction in the world we acquire various high-order expectations that can serve us as premises. In our subsequent reasoning we are windowless monads doing our best to mirror each other, mirror each other mirroring each other, and so on.

Of course I do not imagine that anyone will solve a coordination problem by first acquiring a seventeenth-order expectation from somewhere and then sitting down to do his replications. For one thing, we rarely do have expectations of higher order than, say, fourth. For another thing, any ordinary situation that could justify a high-order expectation would also justify low-order expectations directly, without recourse to nested replications.

All the same, given the needed ancillary premises, an expectation of arbitrarily high order about action does give an agent *one* good reason for a choice of action. The one may, and normally will, be one reason among the many which jointly suffice to justify his choice. Suppose the agent is originally justified somehow in having expectations of several orders about his own and his partners' actions. And suppose the ancillary premises are available. Then each of his original expectations independently gives him a reason to act one way or another. If he is lucky, all these independent reasons will be reasons for the same action.[5] Then that action is strongly, because redundantly, justified; he has more reason to do it than could have been provided by any one of his original expectations by itself.

I said earlier that coordination might be rationally achieved with the aid of concordant mutual expectations about action. We have seen that these may be derived from first- and higher-order expectations about action, preferences, and rationality. So we generalize: coordination may be rationally achieved with the aid of a system of concordant mutual expectations, of first or higher orders, about the agents' actions, preferences, and rationality.

The more orders of expectation about action contribute to an agent's decision, the more independent justifications the agent will have; and insofar as he is aware of those justifications, the more firmly his choice will be determined. Circumstances that will help to solve a coordination problem, therefore, are circumstances in which the agents become justified in forming mutual expectations belonging to a concordant system. And the more orders, the better.

In considering how to solve coordination problems, I have postponed the answer that first comes to mind: by agreement. If the agents can communicate (without excessive cost), they can ensure a common understanding of their problem by discussing it. They can choose a coordination equilibrium—an arbitrary one, or one especially good for some or all of them, or one they can reach without too much

[5] Michael Scriven, in "An Essential Unpredictability in Human Behavior," *Scientific Psychology: Principles and Approaches,* ed. B. B. Wolman (New York: Basic Books, 1965), has discussed mutual replication of practical reasoning between agents in a game of conflict who want *not* to conform to each other's expectations. There is a cyclic alternation: from my $(n + 4)$th-order expectation that I will go to Minsk to my $(n + 3)$th-order expectation that you will go to Pinsk to my $(n + 2)$th-order expectation that I will go to Pinsk to my $(n + 1)$th-order expectation that you will go to Minsk to my nth-order expectation that I will go to Minsk . . . Scriven notices that we cannot both act on complete and accurate replications of each other's reasoning. He takes this to prove human unpredictability. But perhaps it simply proves that the agents cannot both have enough time to finish their replications, since the time either needs increases with the time the other uses. See David Lewis and Jane Richardson, "Scriven on Human Unpredictability," *Philosophical Studies,* 17 (1966), pp. 69–74.

mutual confidence. And each can assure the rest that he will do his part of the chosen equilibrium. Coordination by means of an agreement is not, of course, an alternative to coordination by means of concordant mutual expectations. Rather, agreement is one means of producing those expectations. It is an especially effective means, since it produces strong concordant expectations of several orders.

Suppose you and I want to meet tomorrow; today we happen to meet, and we make an appointment. Each thereby gives evidence of his interest in going where the other goes and of his intention to go to a certain place. By observing this evidence, we form concordant first-order expectations about each other's preferences and action. By observing each other observing it, we may also form concordant second-order expectations. By observing each other observing each other observing it, we may even form concordant third-order expectations. And so on; not forever, of course, but limited by the amount of reasoning we do and the amount we ascribe to each other—perhaps one or two steps more. The result is a system of concordant mutual expectations of several orders, conducive to coordination by means of replication.

The agents' agreement might be an exchange of formal or tacit promises. But it need not be. Even a man whose word is his bond can remove the promissory force by explicit disavowal, if not otherwise. An exchange of declarations of present intention will be good enough, even if each explicitly retains his right to change his plans later. No one need bind himself to act against his own interest. Rather, it will be in the interest of each to do just what he has led the others to expect him to do, since that action will be best for him if the others act on their expectations.

If one does consider himself bound by a promise, he has a second, independent incentive. His payoffs are modified, since he has attached the onus of promise breaking to all but one choice. Indeed, he may modify his payoffs so much by promising that the situation is no longer a coordination problem at all. For instance, the agent's promised action might become his dominant choice: he might wish to keep his promise no matter what, coordination or no coordination.

If such a strong promise is made publicly, the others will know that they must go along with the one who has promised, for they know what he will do. Such forceful promising is a way of getting rid of coordination problems, not a way of solving them.

Explicit agreement is an especially good and common means to coordination—so much so that we are tempted to speak of coordination otherwise produced as *tacit* agreement. But agreement (literally understood) is not the only source of concordant expectations to help us solve our coordination problems. We do without agreement by choice if we find ourselves already satisfied with the content and strength of our mutual expectations. We do without it by necessity if we have no way to communicate, or if we can communicate only at a cost that outweighs our improved chance of coordination (say, if we are conspirators being shadowed).

Schelling has experimented with coordination problems in which the agents cannot communicate. His subjects know only that they share a common understanding of their problem—for instance, they may get instructions describing their problem and stating that everyone gets the same instructions. It turns out that sophisticated subjects in an experimental setting can often do very well—much better than chance—at solving novel coordination problems without communicating. They try for a coordination equilibrium that is somehow *salient*: one that stands out from the rest by its uniqueness in some conspicuous respect. It does not have to be uniquely *good*; indeed, it could be uniquely bad. It merely has to be unique in some way the subjects will notice, expect each other to notice, and so on. If different coordination equilibria are unique in different conspicuous ways, the subjects will need to be alike in the relative importance they attach to different respects of comparison; but often they are enough alike to solve the problem.

How can we explain coordination by salience? The subjects might all tend to pick the salient as a last resort, when they have no stronger ground for choice. Or they might expect each other to have that tendency, and act accordingly; or they might expect each other to expect each other to have that tendency and act accordingly, and act accordingly; and so on. Or—more likely—there might be a mixture of these. Their first- and higher-order expectations of a tendency to pick the salient as a last resort would be a system of concordant expectations capable of producing coordination at the salient equilibrium.

If their expectations did produce coordination, it would not matter whether anyone really would have picked the salient as a last resort. For each would have had a good reason for his choice, so his choice would not have been a last resort.

Thus even in a novel coordination problem—which is an extreme case—the agents can sometimes obtain the concordant expectations they need without communicating. An easier, and more common, case is that of a *familiar* coordination problem without communication. Here the agents' source of mutual expectations is precedent: acquaintance with past solved instances of their present coordination problem.

4. Convention

Let us start with the simplest case of coordination by precedent and generalize in various ways. In this way we shall meet the phenomenon I call *convention*, the subject of this book.

Suppose we have been given a coordination problem, and we have reached some fairly good coordination equilibrium. Given exactly the same problem again, perhaps each of us will repeat what he did before. If so, we will reach the same solution. If you and I met yesterday—by luck, by agreement, by salience, or however—and today we find we must meet again, we might both go back to yesterday's meeting place, each hoping to find the other there. If we were cut off on the telephone and you happened to call back as I waited, then if we are cut off again in the same call, I will wait again.

We can explain the force of precedent just as we explained the force of salience. Indeed, precedent is merely the source of one important kind of salience: conspicuous uniqueness of an equilibrium because we reached it last time. We may tend to repeat the action that succeeded before if we have no strong reason to do otherwise. Whether or not any of us really has this tendency, we may somewhat expect each other to have it, or expect each other to expect each other to have it, and so on—that is, we may each have first- and higher-order expectations that the others will do their parts of the old coordination equilibrium, unless they have reason to act otherwise. Each one's expectation that the others will do their parts, strengthened perhaps by replication using his higher-order expectations, gives him some reason to do his own part. And if his original expectations of some order or other were strong enough, he will have a decisive reason to do his part. So he will do it.

I have been supposing that we are given a coordination problem, and then given the same problem again. But, of course, we could never be given exactly the same problem twice. There must be this difference at least: the second time, we can draw on our experience with the first. More generally, the two problems will differ in several independent respects. We cannot do exactly what we did before. Nothing we could do this time is exactly like what we did before—like it in every respect—because the situations are not exactly alike.

So suppose not that we are given the original problem again, but rather that we are given a new coordination problem analogous somehow to the original one. Guided by whatever analogy we notice, we tend to follow precedent by trying for a coordination equilibrium in the new problem which uniquely corresponds to the one we reached before.

There might be alternative analogies. If so, there is room for ambiguity about what would be following precedent and doing what we did before. Suppose that yesterday I called you on the telephone and I called back when we were cut off. Today you call me and we are cut off. We have a precedent in which I called back and a precedent—the same one—in which the original caller called back. But this time you are the original caller. No matter what I do this time, I do something analogous to what we did before. Our ambiguous precedent does not help us.

In fact, there are always innumerable alternative analogies. Were it not that we happen uniformly to notice some analogies and ignore others—those we call "natural" or "artificial," respectively—precedents would always be completely ambiguous and worthless. *Every* coordination equilibrium in our new problem (every other combination, too) corresponds uniquely to what we did before under *some* analogy, shares *some* distinctive description with it alone. Fortunately, most of the analogies are artificial. We ignore them; we do not tend to let them guide our choice, nor do we expect each other to have any such tendency, nor do we expect each other to expect each other to, and so on. And fortunately we have learned that all of us will mostly notice the same analogies. That is why precedents can be unambiguous in practice, and often are. If we notice only one of the analogies between our problem and the precedent, or if one of those we notice seems far more conspicuous than the others, or even if several are conspicuous but they all happen to agree in indicating the same choice, then the other analogies do not matter. We are not in trouble unless conflicting analogies force themselves on our attention.

The more respects of similarity between the new problem and the precedent, the more likely it is that different analogies will turn out to agree, the less room there will be for ambiguity, and the easier it will be to follow precedent. A precedent in which I, the original caller, called back is ambiguous given a new problem in which you are the original caller—but not given a new problem in which I am again the original caller. That is why I began by pretending that the new problem was like the precedent in all respects.

Salience in general is uniqueness of a coordination equilibrium in a preeminently conspicuous respect. The salience due to precedent is no exception: it is uniqueness of a coordination equilibrium in virtue of its preeminently conspicuous analogy to what was done successfully before.

So far I have been supposing that the agents who set the precedent are the ones who follow it. This made sure that the agents given the second problem were acquainted with the circumstances and outcome of the first, and expected each other to be, expected each other to

expect each other to be, and so on. But it is not an infallible way
and not the only way. For instance, if yesterday I told you a story
about people who got separated in the subway and happened to meet
again at Charles Street, and today we get separated in the same way,
we might independently decide to go and wait at Charles Street. It
makes no difference whether the story I told you was true, or whether
you thought it was, or whether I thought it was, or even whether
I claimed it was. A fictive precedent would be as effective as an actual
one in suggesting a course of action for us, and therefore as good
a source of concordant mutual expectations enabling us to meet. So
let us just stipulate that somehow the agents in the new problem are
acquainted with the precedent, expect each other to be acquainted
with it, and so on.

So far I have been supposing that we have a single precedent to
follow. But we might have several. We might all be acquainted with
a class of previous coordination problems, naturally analogous to our
present problem and to each other, in which analogous coordination
equilibria were reached. This is to say that the agents' actions conformed to some noticeable regularity. Since our present problem is
suitably analogous to the precedents, we can reach a coordination
equilibrium by all conforming to this same regularity. Each of us
wants to conform to it if the others do; he has a *conditional preference*
for conformity. If we do conform, the explanation has the familiar
pattern: we tend to follow precedent, given no particular reason to
do anything else; we expect that tendency in each other; we expect
each other to expect it; and so on. We have our concordant first-
and higher-order expectations, and they enable us to reach a coordination equilibrium.

It does not matter *why* coordination was achieved at analogous
equilibria in the previous cases. Even if it had happened by luck,
we could still follow the precedent set. One likely course of events
would be this: the first case, or the first few, acted as precedent for
the next, those for the next, and so on. Similarly, no matter how our
precedents came about, by following them this time we add this case
to the stock of precedents available henceforth.

Several precedents are better than one, not only because we learn by repetition but also because differences between the precedents help to resolve ambiguity. Even if our present situation bears conflicting natural analogies to any one precedent, maybe only one of these analogies will hold between the precedents; so we will pay attention only to that one. Suppose we know of many cases in which a cut-off telephone call was restored, and in every case it was the original caller who called back. In some cases I was the original caller, in some you were, in some neither of us was. Now we are cut off and I was the original caller. For you to call back would be to do something analogous—under one analogy—to what succeeded in some of the previous cases. But we can ignore that analogy, for under it the precedents disagree.

Once there are many precedents available, without substantial disagreement or ambiguity, it is no longer necessary for all of us to be acquainted with precisely the same ones. It is enough if each of us is acquainted with some agreeing precedents, each expects everyone else to be acquainted with some that agree with his, each expects everyone else to expect everyone else to be acquainted with some precedents that agree with his, etc. It is easy to see how that might happen: if one has often encountered cases in which coordination was achieved in a certain problem by conforming to a certain regularity, and rarely or never encountered cases in which it was not, he is entitled to expect his neighbors to have had much the same experience. If I have driven all around the United States and seen many people driving on the right and never one on the left, I may reasonably infer that almost everyone in the United States drives on the right, and hence that this man driving toward me also has mostly seen people driving on the right—even if he and I have not seen any of the *same* people driving on the right.

Our acquaintance with a precedent need not be very detailed. It is enough to know that one has learned of many cases in which coordination was achieved in a certain problem by conforming to a certain regularity. There is no need to be able to specify the time and place, the agents involved, or any other particulars; no need to be able to recall the cases one by one. I cannot cite precedents one by one in which people drove on the right in the United States; I am not sure I can cite even one case; nonetheless, I know very well that I have often seen cars driven in the United States, and almost always they were on the right. And since I have no reason to think I encountered an abnormal sample, I infer that drivers in the United States do almost always drive on the right; so anyone I meet driving in the United States will believe this just as I do, will expect me to believe it, and so on.

Coordination by precedent, at its simplest, is this: achievement of coordination by means of shared acquaintance with the achievement of coordination in a single past case exactly like our present coordination problem. By removing inessential restrictions, we have come to this: achievement of coordination by means of shared acquaintance with a *regularity* governing the achievement of coordination in a class of past cases which bear some conspicuous analogy to one another and to our present coordination problem. Our acquaintance with this regularity comes from our experience with some of its instances, not necessarily the same ones for everybody.

Given a regularity in past cases, we may reasonably extrapolate it into the (near) future. For we are entitled to expect that when agents acquainted with the past regularity are confronted by an analogous new coordination problem, they will succeed in achieving coordination by following precedent and continuing to conform to the same regularity. We come to expect conforming actions not only in past cases but in future ones as well. We acquire a general belief, unrestricted as to time, that members of a certain population conform to a certain regularity in a certain kind of recurring coordination problem for the sake of coordination.

Each new action in conformity to the regularity adds to our experience of general conformity. Our experience of general conformity in the past leads us, by force of precedent, to expect a like conformity in the future. And our expectation of future conformity is a reason to go on conforming, since to conform if others do is to achieve a coordination equilibrium and to satisfy one's own preferences. And so it goes—we're here because we're here because we're here because we're here. Once the process gets started, we have a metastable self-perpetuating system of preferences, expectations, and actions capable of persisting indefinitely. As long as uniform conformity is a coordination equilibrium, so that each wants to conform conditionally upon conformity by the others, conforming action produces expectation of conforming action and expectation of conforming action produces conforming action.

This is the phenomenon I call convention. Our first, rough, definition is:

> A regularity R in the behavior of members of a population P when they are agents in a recurrent situation S is a *convention* if and only if, in any instance of S among members of P,
>
> (1) everyone conforms to R;
> (2) everyone expects everyone else to conform to R;
> (3) everyone prefers to conform to R on condition that the others do, since S is a coordination problem and uniform conformity to R is a proper coordination equilibrium in S.

5. Sample Conventions

Chapter II will be devoted to improving the definition. But before we hide the concept beneath its refinements, let us see how it applies to examples. Consider some conventions to solve our sample coordination problems.

(1) If you and I must meet every week, perhaps at first we will make a new appointment every time. But after we have met at the same time and place for a few weeks running, one of us will say, "See you here next week," at the end of every meeting. Later still we will not say anything (unless our usual arrangement is going to be unsatisfactory next week). We will just both go regularly to a certain place at a certain time every week, each going there to meet the other and confident that he will show up. This regularity that has gradually developed in our behavior is a convention.

In this case the convention that sets our meeting place holds in the smallest possible population: just two people. In other cases, larger populations—perhaps with changing membership—have conventional meeting places. What makes a soda fountain, coffeehouse, or bar "in" is the existence of a convention in some social circle that it is the place to go when one wants to socialize. The man in the song—"Standing on a corner with a dollar in my hand / Looking for a woman who's looking for a man"— is standing on *that* corner in conformity to a convention among all the local prostitutes and their customers.

(2) In my hometown of Oberlin, Ohio, until recently all local telephone calls were cut off without warning after three minutes. Soon after the practice had begun, a convention grew up among Oberlin residents that when a call was cut off the original caller would call back while the called party waited. Residents usually conformed to this regularity in the expectation of conformity by the other party to the call. In this way calls were easily restored, to the advantage of all concerned. New residents were told about the convention or learned it through experience. It persisted for a decade or so until the cutoff was abolished.

Other regularities might have done almost as well. It could have been the called party who always called back, or the alphabetically first, or even the older. Any of these regularities could have become the convention if enough of us had started conforming to it. It would have been a bit less convenient than our actual convention; if the original caller calls back, he may still remember the number and he must at least know where to find it. But the inconveniences of another convention would not have outweighed the advantage of achieving a coordination equilibrium by calling back if and only if one's partner does not.

This example illustrates the possibility that (describing actions in any natural way) a conventional regularity may specify different actions under different conditions. In this case it specifies what we would naturally call different actions for agents involved in situation *S* in different *roles*. Except for *ad hoc* descriptions like "action in conformity to such-and-such regularity," the actions conforming to a conventional regularity do not have to share any common natural description. Therefore, when we speak of a convention to do an action *A* in a situation *S*, it must be understood that *A* may stand for an unnaturally complex action-description.

(3) If the two rowers in Hume's boat manage somehow to fall into a smooth rhythm and maintain it for a while, they "do it by an agreement or convention, though they have never given promises to each other." A regularity in their behavior—their rowing in that particular rhythm—persists because they expect it to be continued and they want to match their rhythms of rowing. "This common sense of interest . . . known to both . . . produces a suitable resolution and behavior" in which "the actions of each . . . have a reference to those of the other, and are performed upon the supposition that something is to be performed upon the other part."

This convention is peculiar. It holds in a very small population for a very short time—between two people for a few minutes—and the regularity is one we would find it very hard to describe, though we can easily catch on to it. But these oddities do not detract from its conventionality.

(4) We drive in the right lane on roads in the United States (or in the left lane on roads in Britain, Australia, Sweden before 1967, parts of Austria before a certain date, and elsewhere) because we do not want to drive in the same lane as the drivers coming toward us, and we expect them to drive on the right.

There is a complication: if we do not drive on the right, the highway patrol will catch us and we will be punished. So we have an independent incentive to drive on the right, and this second incentive is independent of how the others drive. But it makes no important difference. If I expected the others to be on the left, I would be there too, highway patrol or no highway patrol. My preference for driving on the same side as the others outweighs any incentive the highway patrol may give me to drive on the right. And so it is for almost everyone else, I am sure. The highway patrol modifies the payoffs in favor of driving on the right; but there are still two different coordination equilibria. The punishments are superfluous if they agree with our convention, are outweighed if they go against it, are not decisive either way, and hence do not make it any less conventional to drive on the right. The same goes for other considerations favoring one coordination equilibrium over the other: the fact that our cars have left-hand drive, the fact that we are mostly right-handed, and so on.

(5) If four men who camp together find that often they waste effort by covering the same ground in search of firewood, they may get fed up and agree once and for all: let Morgan look to the north, Jones to the east, Owen to the south, Griffith to the west. From that day on, each goes his proper way without further discussion. A regularity has begun by explicit agreement. At first, perhaps, it persists because each man feels bound by his promise and takes no account of the advantages of keeping it or breaking it. But years pass. They forget that they agreed. Morgan is replaced by Thomas, who never heard of the agreement and never promised anything. Yet whenever they need firewood each still goes off in his proper direction, because he knows that is how to have the ground to himself. As the force of their original promises fades away, the regularity in their behavior becomes a convention.

(6) Wanting to attend parties dressed as the others will be dressed, we wear whatever is conventional dress for the occasion; in picking our clothes we act in conformity to a convention of our social circle. By means of a conditional conventional regularity specifying the style of clothes worn in various circumstances, we satisfy our common interest in being dressed alike.

But we must distinguish two cases. If each of us wants to dress like the majority and wants everyone else to dress like the majority too, then we achieve a coordination equilibrium when we all dress alike: our regularity is a genuine convention. Suppose, however, that many of us are nasty people who want to dress like the majority but also want to have a differently dressed minority to sneer at. We still achieve an equilibrium when we all dress alike, but it is not a coordination equilibrium: nobody wishes he himself had dressed otherwise, but the nasty ones wish that a few other people—say, their worst enemies—had dressed otherwise. The regularity whereby we achieve this equilibrium is not a genuine convention by my definition, because the element of conflict of interest prevents it from being a means of reaching a *coordination* equilibrium.

It may not be obvious that our regularities of dress should not be called conventions if there are many people who want to see them violated. But when our analysis has shown us how the presence of substantial conflict makes a disanalogy between this case and other clear cases of convention, and makes an important analogy between this case and clear cases of nonconvention like the one to be examined in Chapter III.5, I think we ought to end up agreeing with the analysis even against our first impressions. If the reader disagrees, I can only remind him that I did not undertake to analyze anyone's concept of convention but mine.

(7) If we are contented oligopolists who want to maintain a uniform but fluctuating price for our commodity, we dare not make any explicit agreement on prices; that would be a conspiracy in restraint of trade. But we can come to a tacit understanding—that is, a convention—by our ways of responding to each others' prices. We might, for instance, start to follow a price leader: one firm that takes the initiative in changing prices, with due care to set a price in the range that is satisfactory to all of us.

In this example, it becomes seriously artificial to divide our continuous activity into a sequence of separate analogous coordination problems, related only by force of precedent. (The difficulty will reappear in examples [9], [10], and [11]; it was present somewhat in [3] and [4].) We can actually set or reconsider prices at any time. How long is a coordination problem? Pretend, already idealizing, that we set our prices every morning and cannot change them later in the day. Then each business day is a coordination problem. But a day is too short. Our customers take more than a day to shop around;

they compare my price for today with yours for yesterday and some-one else's for tomorrow. We are leaving out most of the coordination: coordination of one's action on one day with another's action on another nearby day. If, on the other hand, we take longer stretches as the coordination problems, then—contrary to the definition—every-one has time for several different choices within a single coordination problem. We might pretend that everyone starts each week by choos-ing a contingency plan specifying what to do in every possible circum-stance during the week (a *strategy* in the sense of the theory of games), and then follows his plan all week without making any further choice. Then a business week is a coordination problem in which everyone makes only his one initial choice of a contingency plan. But this treatment badly misdescribes what we do; and it still leaves out the coordination between, say, my prices for Friday and yours for next Monday. A better remedy, scheduled for Chapter II.3, goes deep. We can forget about individual coordination problems; instead of saying that uniform conformity to a regularity R constitutes a coordina-tion equilibrium in every instance of a situation S, we can say approx-imately the same thing in terms of conditional preferences for conform-ity to R.

(8) If Rousseau's stag hunters stay with the hunt every time, they do so by a convention. Each stays because he trusts the others to stay as they did before, and he will eat better by staying and taking his share of the stag when it is caught.

But, less obviously, if they always split up and catch rabbits sep-arately, that is a convention too. If the stag hunt fails unless all take part, there is no point in joining unless all the others do. Each prefers to catch rabbits if even one of the others does, and *a fortiori* if all the others do. For each to catch his rabbit is not a good coordination equilibrium. But it is a coordination equilibrium nonetheless, so long as catching a rabbit is better than going off on a one-man stag hunt that is bound to fail. So rabbit catching is, by definition, a conven-tion.

(9) On the hypothesis that each of us wants the exclusive use of

some land and that nobody ever thinks it worth the trouble to try taking over the use of some land from another, any *de facto* division of the land is a convention. Each goes on using a certain portion and keeping off the rest in the knowledge that, since others will go on using everything else, that is the only way he can meet his needs and stay out of trouble. A better convention might provide a regular way to deal with changes in the population of land users. It might be part of the convention, for instance, that when any man dies, the oldest boy not yet using land begins to use the vacant portion.

I have not called these portions of land *property*. At its simplest—say, among anarchists—the institution of property might be nothing more than a convention specifying who shall have the exclusive use of which goods. This seems to be Hume's theory of property. For us, the institution of property is more complicated; we have built it into an elaborate system of laws and institutions. We do not say that a squatter owns the land he farms, though he enjoys the exclusive use of it by a convention, since another claimant is entitled by law to call on the police to kick the squatter off. I therefore shall not *define* property as goods reserved by convention for someone's exclusive use.

(10) A medium of exchange—say, coin of the realm—has its special status by a convention among tradesmen to take it without question in return for goods and services. Some conventional media are better than others: bulky or perishable ones are bad; ones that would retain some use if the convention collapsed are good—but the inconvenience of accepting a bad medium of exchange is less than the inconvenience of refusing it when others take it, or of taking what one can neither use nor spend. Again, as in (4), there is the complication of legal sanctions. Refusal to accept legal tender makes a debt legally unenforceable. But again, such sanctions are superflous if they agree with convention, are outweighed if they go against it, are not decisive either way, and therefore do not make our regularity any the less conventional.

I suppose we may safely define a *medium of exchange* as any good that is conventionally accepted in some population in return for goods and services. This definition raises an annoying question: is it right to say that we have a convention to accept our media of exchange in return for goods and services? It is false to say that our convention is that we accept our media of exchange in return for goods and services. For what follows "that" does not state any convention because it is true, by definition, of any population. On the other hand, it is true to say *of* our media of exchange that our convention is that we accept *them* in return for goods and services. My question was ambiguous. It can be read opaquely or transparently.[6] It is like the question whether Hegel knew that the number of planets is greater than seven. He did not know that the number of planets is greater than seven. But he did know, *of* the number of planets—namely nine—that *it* is greater than seven.

(11) A population's common use of some one language—Welsh, say—is a convention. The Welshmen in parts of Wales use Welsh; each uses Welsh because he expects his neighbors to, and for the sake of communication he wishes to use whatever language his neighbors use.

Does he not rather wish to use whatever language his neighbors will *understand?* Yes; but as a fact of human nature, he and his neighbors will best understand the language they use. So the right thing to say is that he wishes to use the language they use *because* that is the language they will understand. It follows that this is another case of coordination over time: he wishes to use the language they have been using most over a period in the past, a period long enough for them to have become skilled in its use.

To say that he wishes to use whichever language his neighbors use is not to say that if they switch suddenly, somehow, he would wish to switch immediately. He would not wish to, because he could not; he would have to practice their new language. Besides, he could count on them to understand Welsh for a time after they had ceased to

---

[6] See W. V. Quine, "Quantifiers and Propositional Attitudes," *Journal of Philosophy,* 53 (1956), pp. 177–187.

use it. But probably he would wish to switch as soon as he easily could. And if it suddenly came to pass that his neighbors had been using their new language for twenty years—while he, let us say, had been sleeping like Rip Van Winkle—he would try to conform with the utmost urgency.

I do not deny, of course, that a man may prefer one language to another—say, the language of his fathers to the language of their conquerors. But that does not matter. Different coordination equilibria do not have to be equally good—only good enough so that everyone is ready to do his part if the others do. There are few who would give up communication out of piety to the mother tongue, if it came to that.

Certainly not every feature of a language is conventional. No humanly possible language relies on ultrasonic whistles, so it is not by convention that the Welshmen do not. We do not yet know exactly which features of languages are conventional and which are common to all humanly possible languages; Noam Chomsky and his school have argued that there is less conventionality than one might have thought.[7] But so long as even two languages are humanly possible, it must be by convention that a population chooses to use one or the other.

In saying that Welshmen use Welsh by convention, I do not say it is a convention that Welshmen use Welsh. This, or something similar but more complicated, might perhaps be true by definition of "Welsh." Rather, I say *of* Welsh that it is a convention among Welshmen that *they* use *it*. The difference is the same ambiguity between opaque and transparent readings that arose in (10).

If using Welsh is to be a convention, it must be a regularity in behavior. It is not, of course, a regularity that fully determines a Welshman's behavior. He can say a variety of things, or remain silent, and he can respond to utterances in a variety of ways, and still be conforming to the conventional regularity. But that is nothing special.

[7] Noam Chomsky, "Recent Contributions to the Theory of Innate Ideas," *Synthese,* 17 (1967), pp. 2–11.

No convention determines every detail of behavior. (The meeting-place convention, for instance, does not specify whether to walk or ride to the meeting place.) This convention, like any other, restricts behavior without removing all choice. There is more choice, and more important choice, in this case than in some others; but there is no difference in kind.

A convention is a regularity in behavior. I do not want to say that the users of Welsh are conforming to their convention when and only when they are rightly said to be "using Welsh." A man lying in Welsh is using Welsh, but he is violating its convention; a man who remains silent during a conversation may be conforming to the convention although he is not using Welsh. In due course we shall see how the convention of a language may be described; here I will say only that it is a regularity restricting one's production of, and response to, verbal utterances and inscriptions. Linguistic competence consists in part of a disposition to conform to that restriction with ease; and in part of an expectation that one's neighbors will be likewise disposed, with a recognition of their conformity as the reason for one's own. No doubt a child or an idiot may conform without reason; if so, he is not party to the convention and his linguistic competence is incomplete.

II | Convention Refined

1. Common Knowledge

Agreement, salience, or precedent, we have seen, can solve a coordination problem by producing a system of concordant first- and higher-order mutual expectations. We need only imagine cases to convince ourselves that higher-order expectations *would* be produced. But how? What premises have we to justify us in concluding that others have certain expectations, that others expect others to have certain expectations, and so on? And how is the process cut off—as it surely is—so that it produces only expectations of the first few orders?

Take a simple case of coordination by agreement. Suppose the following state of affairs—call it *A*—holds: you and I have met, we have been talking together, you must leave before our business is done; so you say you will return to the same place tomorrow. Imagine the case. Clearly, I will expect you to return. You will expect me to expect you to return. I will expect you to expect me to expect you to return. Perhaps there will be one or two orders more.

What is it about *A* that explains the generation of these higher-order expectations? I suggest the reason is that *A* meets these three conditions:

(1) You and I have reason to believe that *A* holds.
(2) *A* indicates to both of us that you and I have reason to believe that *A* holds.
(3) *A* indicates to both of us that you will return.

What is indicating? Let us say that *A* *indicates* to someone *x* that

_____ if and only if, if x had reason to believe that A held, x would thereby have reason to believe that _____. What A indicates to x will depend, therefore, on x's inductive standards and background information.

The three main premises (1), (2), (3), together with suitable ancillary premises regarding our rationality, inductive standards, and background information, suffice to justify my higher-order expectations. Let us see how my reasoning would work.

Consider that if A indicates something to x, and if y shares x's inductive standards and background information, then A must indicate the same thing to y. Therefore, if A indicates to x that y has reason to believe that A holds, and if A indicates to x that _____, and if x has reason to believe that y shares x's inductive standards and background information, then A indicates to x that y has reason to believe that _____ (this reason being y's reason to believe that A holds). Suppose you and I do have reason to believe we share the same inductive standards and background information, at least nearly enough so that A will indicate the same things to both of us. Then (2) applied to (3) implies:

(4) A indicates to both of us that each of us has reason to believe that you will return.

And (2) applied in turn to (4) implies:

(5) A indicates to both of us that each of us has reason to believe that the other has reason to believe that you will return.

And so on *ad infinitum*, since each new conclusion begins "A indicates to both of us that . . ." Note that this is a chain of implications, not of steps in anyone's actual reasoning. Therefore there is nothing improper about its infinite length. Figure 26 is a more detailed representation of these implications in my case; those in your case could be represented similarly.

Consider next that our definition of indication yields a principle of detatchment: if A indicates to x that _____ and x has reason to

I believe that you
share my inductive
standards and back-
ground information

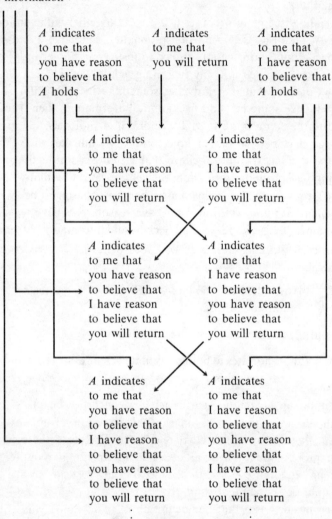

Figure 26

believe that A holds, then x has reason to believe that ____ . Premise (1) applied in this way to (3) implies:

(3′) Each of us has reason to believe that you will return.

Premise (1) applied to (4) implies:

(4′) Each of us has reason to believe that the other has reason to believe that you will return.

Premise (1) applied to (5) implies:

(5′) Each of us has reason to believe that the other has reason to believe that the first has reason to believe that you will return.

And so on, for the whole infinite sequence we considered above. I am still not talking about anyone's actual reasoning or what anyone actually does believe. But the only actual reasoning needed now is reasoning to convert these iterations of "has reason to believe" to the corresponding iterations of "does believe." For that we need ancillary premises about rationality.

Anyone who has reason to believe something will come to believe it, provided he has a sufficient degree of rationality. So according to (3′), if we both have a sufficient degree of rationality, then it will come to be that

(3″) Each of us expects that you will return.

According to (4′), if each of us has reason to ascribe a sufficient degree of rationality to the other, then each has reason to expect that the other expects that you will return. If, in addition, we both have a sufficient degree of rationality, then it will come to be that

(4″) Each of us expects that the other expects that you will return.

According to (5′), if each of us has reason to expect that the other has reason to ascribe a sufficient degree of rationality to him, then each has reason to expect that the other has reason to expect that he expects that you will return. If, in addition, each of us has reason to ascribe a sufficient degree of rationality to the other, then each has reason to expect that the other expects that he expects that you will return. And if, in addition, we both have a sufficient degree of rationality, then it will come to be that

> (5″) Each of us expects that the other expects that he expects that you will return.

And so on. Each term of the sequence (3′), (4′), (5′) . . . , together with sufficient rationality, reason to ascribe sufficient rationality, etc., guarantees formation of the corresponding first- or higher-order expectation. But the degrees of rationality we are required to have, to have reason to ascribe, etc., obviously increase quickly. That is why expectations of only the first few orders are actually formed. The generating process stops when the ancillary premises give out.

This completes our example of a state of affairs which produces higher-order expectations. I take this example to be typical; all the higher-order expectations involved in sustaining conventions, and more or less all we ever have, seem to be produced in this way.

Let us say that it is *common knowledge* in a population P that ___ if and only if some state of affairs A holds such that:

> (1) Everyone in P has reason to believe that A holds.
> (2) A indicates to everyone in P that everyone in P has reason to believe that A holds.
> (3) A indicates to everyone in P that ___.

We can call any such state of affairs A a *basis* for common knowledge in P that ___. A provides the members of P with part of what they need to form expectations of arbitrarily high order, regarding sequences of members of P, that ___. The part it gives them is the part peculiar to the content ___. The rest of what they need is what they need to form *any* higher-order expectations in the way we are considering: mutual ascription of some common inductive standards and background information, rationality, mutual ascription of rationality, and so on.

Let us return to our example and consider the state of affairs A more completely. Suppose that as part of A we manifest our conditional preferences for returning to the meeting place. Then A may also indicate to us that we both have such preferences. If so, A can serve as a basis not only for common knowledge that you will return, but also as a basis for common knowledge that each of us prefers to return if the other does. Suppose also that as part of A we somehow manifest a modicum of rationality. Then A may indicate to us, and be a basis for common knowledge of, our possession of this modicum of rationality. By now A—our incident of agreeing to return—is generating all the higher-order expectations that contribute to our success in solving our coordination problem by means of replication.

A basis for common knowledge generates higher-order expectations with the aid of pre-existing higher-order expectations of rationality. Can these themselves be generated by some basis for common knowledge? Yes, because all the higher-order expectations of rationality needed to generate an nth-order expectation are themselves of less than nth-order. What cuts off the generation of higher-order expectations is the limited amount of rationality indicated by any basis—not any difficulty in generating higher-order expectations of as much rationality as *is* indicated by a basis.

Agreement to do one's part of a coordination equilibrium is a basis for common knowledge that everyone will do his part. Salience is another basis for common knowledge that everyone will do his part of a coordination equilibrium; but it is a weaker basis, in general, and generates weaker higher-order expectations, since the salience of an equilibrium is not a very strong indication that agents will tend to choose it. Precedents also are a basis for common knowledge that everyone will do his part of a coordination equilibrium; and, in particular, past conformity to a convention is a basis for common knowledge of a tendency to go on conforming. Consider a conventional regularity R in a population P. Everyone in P has reason to believe that members of P have conformed to R in the past. The fact that members of P have conformed to R in the past indicates to everyone in P that everyone in P has reason to believe that members of P have conformed to R in the past. And the fact that members of P have conformed to R in the past indicates to everyone in P that they will tend to do so in the future as well.

For example, drivers in the United States have hitherto driven on the right. All of us have reason to believe that this is so. And the fact that this is so indicates to all of us that all of us have reason to believe that drivers in the United States have hitherto driven on the right and also that drivers in the United States will tend to drive on the right henceforth.

Our defining conditions for the existence of a convention consist of a regularity in behavior, a system of mutual expectations, and a system of preferences. I propose to amend the definition: not only must these conditions be satisfied, but also it must be common knowledge in the population that they are. Our amended definition is:

> A regularity R in the behavior of members of a population P when they are agents in a recurrent situation S is a *convention* if and only if it is true that, and it is common knowledge in P that, in any instance of S among members of P,
>
> (1) everyone conforms to R;
> (2) everyone expects everyone else to conform to R;
> (3) everyone prefers to conform to R on condition that the others do, since S is a coordination problem and uniform conformity to R is a coordination equilibrium in S.

Thus there is to be some state of affairs A (such that A holds, everyone in P has reason to believe that A holds, and A indicates to everyone in P that everyone in P has reason to believe that A holds) which indicates to everyone in P that members of P conform to R, that they expect each other to conform to R, and that they have preferences which make uniform conformity to R a coordination equilibrium.

One reason to amend the definition of convention is simply that we want to write into the definition all of the important features common to our examples, and common knowledge of the relevant facts seems to be one such feature. There is another reason: the amendment helps to deal with certain odd cases, regularities which seem intuitively unlike clear cases of convention but which would have qualified as conventions under the unamended definition.

Suppose everyone drives on the right because he expects everyone else to drive on the right and he wants to prevent collisions. But suppose no one gives anyone else credit for intelligence equal to his own. Everyone holds this false belief (call it f): "Except for myself, everyone drives on the right by habit, for no reason, and would go on driving on the right no matter what he expected others to do." This is a case of convention under the unamended definition, despite the false beliefs; but I think it ought to be excluded. It cannot be a case of convention under the amended definition (unless we are extremely irrational); for if it is, there is some state of affairs which we have reason to believe holds and which indicates to us that f is false. This case is only the first of a sequence. Suppose next that no one really has the false belief f, but everyone falsely ascribes it to everyone else. This too cannot be a case of convention under the amended definition (unless we are extremely irrational); for if it is, there is some state of affairs which we have reason to believe holds and which indicates to us that everyone has reason to disbelieve f. And so on. The cases become more and more unlikely, but no less deserving of exclusion; the amended definition continues to exclude them (given a sufficiently strong assumption of rationality—stronger and stronger assumptions of rationality are needed as we go on).

By now one might guess that common knowledge is the only possible source of higher-order expectations. But it is not; there is a general method for producing expectations of arbitrarily high order in isolation. For instance, I can acquire an isolated fourth-order expectation as follows. Suppose I am a resident of Ableton and I believe everything printed in the *Ableton Argus*. Today's *Argus* prints this story:

> The *Bakerville Bugle* is totally unreliable; what it prints is as likely to be false as to be true. Yet the residents of Bakerville believe everything in it. Today's *Bugle* printed this story:
>
>> The *Charlie City Crier* is totally unreliable; what it prints is as likely to be false as to be true. Yet the residents of Charlie City believe everything in it. Today's *Crier* printed this story:
>>
>>> The *Dogpatch Daily* is totally unreliable; what it prints is as likely to be false as to be true. Yet the residents of Dogpatch believe everything in it. Today's *Daily* printed this story:
>>>
>>>> Tomorrow it will rain cats and dogs.

I should not expect it to rain cats and dogs. I should not expect the residents of Dogpatch to expect it to rain cats and dogs. I should not expect the residents of Charlie City to expect the residents of Dogpatch to expect it to rain cats and dogs. But I should expect the residents of Bakerville to expect the residents of Charlie City to expect the residents of Dogpatch to expect it to rain cats and dogs. In other words, I should have a fourth-order expectation that it will rain cats and dogs, without any corresponding lower-order expectations that it will. Obviously, the method would have worked for an arbitrarily long sequence of newspapers; the sequence could have repeated, provided no two adjacent terms were the same. I do not claim that this method of generating isolated higher-order expectations is of much practical importance; it merely establishes the possibility.

2. Knowledge of Conventions

Suppose it is common knowledge in a population P that some state of affairs B holds. Then everyone in P has reason to expect it to be common knowledge in P that B holds. For by definition of common knowledge, there is some state of affairs A such that:

(1) Everyone in P has reason to believe that A holds;
(2) A indicates in P that everyone in P has reason to believe that A holds;
(3) A indicates in P that B holds.

From (1) and (2) we may infer:

(4) Everyone in P has reason to believe that everyone in P has reason to believe that A holds.

From (2) by itself we may infer:

(5) Everyone in P has reason to believe that A indicates in P that everyone in P has reason to believe that A holds.

Likewise from (3) we may infer:

(6) Everyone in P has reason to believe that A indicates in P that B holds.

And from (4), (5), and (6) we may infer that everyone in P has reason to believe that there is a state of affairs A which satisfies conditions (1), (2), and (3).

So if a convention, in particular, holds as an item of common knowledge, then to belong to the population in which that convention holds—to be party to it—is to know, in some sense, that it holds. If a regularity R is a convention in population P, then it must be true, and common knowledge in P, that R satisfies the defining conditions for a convention. If it is common knowledge that R satisfies them, then everyone in P has reason to believe that it is true, and common knowledge in P, that R satisfies them; which is to say that everyone in P must have reason to believe that R is a convention.

This is not to say that a party to the convention has any special, infallible way of acquiring his knowledge. But he must *have acquired* it somehow, in an ordinary way, in order to be one of those among

If a convention is common knowledge, then to belong to the group that follows it you must know it whom the convention holds. Discovery of the convention is the principal part of one's initiation into it.

Consider the conventions of language, whatever they may be. Anyone who is a member of a population *P*, and party to its conventions of language, must know what those conventions are. If any regularity *R* is in fact a convention of language in *P*, any normal[1] member of *P* must have reason to believe that *R* satisfies the defining conditions for a convention.

Here is a vindication of sorts for Stanley Cavell's doctrine that a native speaker has no need of evidence to justify what he says about what he would say. Take a philosopher who claims we would not call an action voluntary if it were not abnormal. He need not cite occasions on which people have failed to call normal actions voluntary, for he is a native speaker of the language he is telling us about. Why is he excused? Not because he, as a native speaker, has some peculiar and infallible way of acquiring his knowledge of his language. And not because his knowledge of what we would say is not real knowledge, as Cavell seems to think when he says, "the native speaker can rely on his own nose; if not, there would be nothing to count." For the man who says what we would say is *not* just speaking for himself.[2]

Rather, it is because the knowledge Cavell has in mind is the speaker's knowledge of conventions to which he himself is a party. When Cavell speaks of our knowledge of "what we would say," I take it he means our knowledge of what we *could* say—could say without violating our conventions of language. He does not mean our knowledge of what we would say in order to provide our audience with the information they want; of what we would say in order not to be rude or boring; of what we would say in order not to divulge trade secrets; of what we would say in order not to twist our tongues.

[1] Not counting children and the feeble-minded, who may conform to *R* without expecting conformity and without preferring to conform conditionally upon the conformity of others.

[2] "Must We Mean What We Say?" *Ordinary Language: Essays in Philosophical Method,* ed. Vere Chappell (Englewood Cliffs, New Jersey: Prentice-Hall, 1964), pp. 75–112.

native speaker does not need to provide evidence to support his claims about what "people say"

Once we have acknowledged that someone is a native speaker of our language, we have already granted that he is party to our conventions. Therefore he knows what those conventions prescribe; he knows "what we would say" in the sense in question. If we turn around and ask him to produce evidence for what he says about what we would say, we challenge his status as a native speaker and as a party to the conventions. We do not challenge some further status he might claim as an authority on the conventions *as well as* a party to them. He has evidence—perfectly ordinary evidence. But if we ask him to show it, we question his membership in the linguistic community to which he purports to belong. It makes no sense *both* to demand evidence for what he says about conventions *and* to take for granted that he is party to those conventions.

This vindication of Cavell's doctrine is a poor sort of vindication, however, because our knowledge of our conventions—that minimum of knowledge everyone has in virtue of his own participation—may be quite a poor sort of knowledge: 3 reasons

(1) It may be merely potential knowledge. We must have evidence from which we could reach the conclusion that any of our conventions meets the defining conditions for a convention, but we may not have done the reasoning to reach the conclusion. If asked whether something is a convention, we might give a snap judgment instead of evaluating our evidence; so we might get the wrong answer.

(2) It may be irremediably nonverbal knowledge. We recall the rowers in Hume's boat, example (3) of Chapter I.5. If I am one of the rowers who row in a certain rhythm by a tacit and temporary convention, I have evidence that we have a convention to row in that rhythm. Our success in rowing in that rhythm for the last few strokes is evidence by which I arrive at my expectation that you will continue to row thus; that you prefer to row thus if I do; and that you expect me to go on rowing thus. And it is evidence that you observe this same evidence. I can use such evidence, I can expect you to use it, and so on; but I cannot describe it. I cannot say how we are rowing— say, one stroke every 2.3 seconds—but I can keep on rowing that way; I can tell whether you keep on rowing that way; later, I could

probably demonstrate to somebody what rhythm it was; I would be surprised if you began to row differently; and so on. Now there *is* a description that can identify the way we are rowing. We take 1.4 ± .05 seconds for the stroke and .9 ± .1 for the return, exerting a peak force of 70 ± 10 pounds near the beginning of each stroke, moving the oars from 32° ± 6° forward to 29° ± 4° back, and so on, in as much detail as you please. But, as we row, we have no use for this sort of description. We can neither give it nor tell whether it is true if somehow it is given. We would need instruments, and even if we had them we could not go on rowing as we were while we took the measurements.

Like it or not, we have plenty of knowledge we cannot put into words. And plenty of our knowledge, in words or not, is based on evidence we cannot hope to report. Our beliefs are formed under the influence of impressions left by a body of past experience, but it is only occasionally that these impressions allow us to report the experience that created them. You probably believe that Kamchatka exists. Your belief is justified, for it is based on evidence: mostly your exposure to various books and to incidents that confirm the reliability of such books. Try, then, to make a convincing case for the existence of Kamchatka by reporting parts of your experience. There is no reason why our knowledge of our conventions should be especially privileged. Like any other knowledge we have, it can be tacit, or based on tacitly known evidence, or both.

(3) It may be knowledge confined to particular instances, taken one at a time. A regularity is conventional in virtue of certain general expectations and preferences regarding conformity to it. But these will not have to be general *in sensu composito;* generality *in sensu diviso* will suffice.

The distinction, Abelard's, is this. If I expect every driver to keep right, *in sensu composito*, then I have one expectation with general content: I expect *that* every driver will keep right. It does not follow that if Jones is a driver, I expect that *he* will keep right, for I might not realize he is a driver. Indeed, I might even realize that Jones is a driver and still not expect that *he* will keep right, for I might

diviso proper sort of knowledge

fail to draw the proper conclusion from my general expectation. If, on the other hand, I expect every driver to keep right, *in sensu diviso*, then I have many expectations, each with *non*general content. I expect *of* Jones, a driver, that *he* will keep right. Of Morgan, too. And so on, for all the drivers there are. I need not know that Jones, Morgan, and the rest are all the drivers there are; I might falsely believe there are other drivers who do not keep right. Or I might altogether lack the general concept of a driver. Generality *in sensu composito* and generality *in sensu diviso* are compatible and often coexist; but it is possible to have either one without the other.

Generality *in sensu diviso* is problematic because expectation and the like apply fundamentally to states of affairs. If I expect that each driver will keep right, I do expect a state of affairs: each driver will keep right. But if I expect, *of* each driver, that *he* will keep right, what states of affairs do I expect? "*He* will keep right" does not specify *any* state of affairs until the pronoun has been replaced by some sort of description—verbal, pictorial, or otherwise—of the person in question. Suppose the description, "the driver of the puce Cadillac ahead of me," fits *x*. Then I can expect *of x* that *he* will keep right by having an expectation which attaches to *x* through that description of him: I expect that the driver of the puce Cadillac ahead of me will keep right. In that case, there is a state of affairs I expect. But not just any description of *x* will do. Suppose, unknown to me, *x* happens to be the chief of police and also the town drunk. I do not expect *of x* that *he* will keep right just because I expect that the chief of police will keep right. I do not fail to expect *of x* that *he* will keep right just because I do not expect that the town drunk will keep right. My expectation needs to be attached to *x* by a description of some special sort; and it is hard to say which descriptions will do, and why.[3]

Consider the general case: I expect every member of *P* involved

---

[3] See Quine, "Quantifiers and Propositional Attitudes"; Richard Montague and Donald Kalish, "'That'," *Philosophical Studies,* 10 (1959), pp. 54–61; David Lewis, "Counterpart Theory and Quantified Modal Logic," *Journal of Philosophy,* 65 (1968), pp. 113–126; David Kaplan, "Quantifying In," *Synthese,* in press.

diviso problematii

with me in an instance of S to conform to R. We have two universal quantifications: one over instances of S, another over members of P involved in any one instance. It is possible, of course, for my expectation to be general *in sensu diviso* over instances of S, but general *in sensu composito* over agents in any one instance. That is, it might be that I expect of any instance of S in which I am involved that everyone in it will conform to R. (Of course it is not possible for my expectation to be general *in sensu composito* over instances and *in sensu diviso* over agents.)

The same distinction between kinds of generality applies to other attitudes. Take our conditional preferences for conformity to convention—say, my preference for conforming to R in instances of S among members of P. If my preference is general *in sensu composito* over instances of S, then I prefer the state of affairs in which I conform to R whenever I am involved in an instance of S (among members of P who conform to R) to the state of affairs in which I sometimes fail to conform to R when I am involved in an instance of S (among members of P who conform to R). But if my preference is general *in sensu diviso*, then for any instance of S (among members of P) in which I am involved, I prefer the state of affairs in which I and the others conform to R in that instance to the state of affairs in which the others conform to R in that instance but I do not. Again the two kinds of generality can and often do coexist, but they are independent.

Which kind of generality over instances of S is wanted in the definition of convention? I should say: whichever kind it is that ensures the agent's ability to apply his general attitudes to the instance at hand. And that is a limited generality *in sensu diviso*. Whenever the agent finds himself in an instance of S among members of P, he must expect the others to conform to R *in that instance*, prefer to conform to R if they do *in that instance*, and so on, in order that he may have reason to conform to R himself. Attitudes general *in sensu composito* would be a likely and welcome addition, and could serve as a source of attitudes general *in sensu diviso*. But they would

expand on two types of generality

Diviso best kind for convention. Composito not enough. But didn't we just say diviso is a poor sort of knowledge?

not be enough by themselves; the agent would have to be able to recognize instances of S and derive the proper particular attitudes. If he did, his attitudes—or at least his propensity to acquire attitudes—would be general *in sensu diviso*.

We can imagine how a convention R regarding action in S might hold in a population P of creatures incapable of having any attitudes general *in sensu composito*. They learn from experience not by coming to believe generalizations, but by acquiring propensities to come up with the right particular beliefs regarding any new case that is presented in sufficient detail. They are exposed to precedents: what we would call (but they could not) instances of S, in which outcomes satisfactory to all concerned were reached by what we would call (but they could not) conformity to R. Thereafter, whenever one of them is presented with a new instance of S, even one not quite like any precedent, he has all the proper attitudes regarding that instance. He expects each other agent involved to do something we would call (but he could not) conformity to R. Considering any two outcomes, he has a preference; and his system of preferences between outcomes is such that there is a coordination equilibrium in which all concerned conform to R. Finally, it is common knowledge among members of P that these attitudes are present in each who is involved in *this particular* instance of S. There is a state of affairs A such that, for this or any other instance of S, for each one involved therein, A indicates that he has the appropriate attitudes in that instance.

Such a creature has a convention and knows it to this extent: given any instance of S, he knows how he and each of his fellows would act therein (namely, in some way that we would call conformity to R). And he knows that they do so by convention; that is, given any of the defining conditions of convention as applied to a given agent in the given situation, he knows the condition is satisfied. But he cannot think of more than one instance—the given one—at a time. He has no general concept of an instance of S, of a member of P, or of an action in conformity to R.

Suppose we who *do* generalize want to exploit this creature's

Where convention relies on diviso + not composito
people cannot articulate the generalization,
yet they act as if there was one. ??

knowledge of his convention, in order to give a general description of that convention. We will have to proceed by trial and error, thinking up hypotheses and trying them out on him in one (well-chosen) instance after another until we think we can predict his response to any future instance.

Even we who could know our own conventions generally *in sensu composito* might happen to know them only generally *in sensu diviso*. If we wanted to know them generally *in sensu composito* as well, we would have to resort to the same sort of trial and error, with ourselves as subjects. Our data about instances of our own conventions would be reliable. But our general hypotheses to systematize those data would be ordinary tentative hypotheses with no privileged status.

acquire in sensu composito from divino by question

3. Alternatives to Conventions

One of my defining conditions for the conventionality of a regularity *R* regarding choice of action by agents in a situation *S* has been:

> In any instance of *S* among members of *P*, everyone prefers to conform to *R* on condition that the others do, since *S* is a coordination problem and uniform conformity to *R* is a coordination equilibrium in *S*.

In the discussion of example (7) in Chapter I.5, we found this condition unsatisfactory whenever we had coordination between actions in nearby instances of *S* within some continuous activity, not just coordination between actions in any one instance of *S*. And we saw that the remedy was not to take longer stretches of activity as our coordination problems, for longer stretches are not coordination problems. Here I shall state new conditions that differ from the old one only by not requiring our activity to be chopped up into self-contained coordination problems. Our new conditions will not imply that *S* is a self-contained problem of interdependent decision, in which each agent involved makes one choice of action and the outcome for each depends on the actions of all; but it will imply that *if* S is that, *then* S is a coordination problem and uniform conformity to R is a coordination equilibrium in S. The special case of a sequence of coordination problems will be covered as before; but we shall find that we have taken care of the other cases at the same time.

First, we require that each agent involved in an instance of S prefers to conform to R conditionally upon conformity by the others involved with him in S. He prefers uniform conformity to R to any combination of actions in which the rest conform and he does not. If S is a self-contained problem of interdependent decision, this first requirement makes uniform conformity to R an equilibrium. Otherwise, uniform conformity is not an equilibrium but something closely resembling one.

Second, we require that all agents involved have approximately the same preferences regarding combinations of their actions, so that S is a situation in which coincidence of interests predominates. In particular, we require that all share the conditional preference of each for his conformity to R. That is, just as I prefer to conform if you and the others do, you also prefer me to conform if you and the others do. Taking this and the first condition together: each prefers that everyone conform to R, on condition that at least all but one conform to R, whether that one is himself or someone else. If S is a self-contained problem of interdependent decision, this second requirement makes uniform conformity to R a proper coordination equilibrium.

Finally, we require that there is a second possible regularity R' (regarding choice of action by agents in S) which meets the same conditions we are imposing on R. We call R' an *alternative* to R. It is enough to require R' to meet the first and second conditions imposed on R. The third is automatic: if R has R' as an alternative, then R' has R itself as an alternative. If S is a self-contained problem of interdependent decision, this last requirement makes uniform conformity to R' a second proper coordination equilibrium. Thereby it ensures that S meets the last condition defining a coordination problem: possession of two or more proper coordination equilibria.

Recall the discussion in Chapter I.2 of the triviality of any situation with a unique coordination equilibrium and predominantly coincident interests. We are now in a better position to describe this triviality: common knowledge of rationality is all it takes for an agent to have reason to do his part of the one coordination equilibrium. He has no need to appeal to precedents or any other source of further mutual expectations.

So far we have protected convention against this triviality by requiring S to be a coordination problem and hence, by definition, to have more than one proper coordination equilibrium. Now that we no longer require S to be a coordination problem, our requirement for an alternative continues the same policy. In fact, whenever S is a self-contained problem of interdependent decision, we have made no change at all.

Our new condition does serve to make evident one property of conventions that was not emphasized before: there is no such thing as the only possible convention. If R is our actual convention, R must have the alternative R', and R' must be such that it could have been our convention instead of R, if only people had started off conforming to R' and expecting each other to. This is why it is redundant to speak of an arbitrary convention. Any convention is arbitrary because there is an alternative regularity that could have been our convention instead. A convention that is *not* arbitrary, so to speak, is a regularity whereby we achieve unique coordination equilibria. Because it is not arbitrary, it does not have to be conventional either. We would conform to it simply because that is the best thing to do. No matter what we had been doing in the past, a failure to conform to the "nonarbitrary convention" could only be a strategic error (or compensation for someone else's anticipated strategic error, or compensation for someone else's anticipated compensation, etc.).

When we try to state the requirement for an alternative more carefully, a question arises. R and R' are supposed to be different, which is to say that action in conformity to R (by an agent in S) is not also in conformity to R', and vice versa. But different always, or different sometimes? After all, instances of S do not have to be exactly alike. They merely have to be analogous, to fall under some common description that is natural enough to allow common knowledge of a propensity to extrapolate from some instances of S to others. So action in conformity to R might also be in conformity to R' for some agents in some instances of S, though not for all.

It is not good enough to require an alternative R' differing from R merely to the extent of being incompatible with R for some, or even for all, agents in some possible instances. Suppose S occurs in a frequent version, shown in Figure 27, and in a rare version, shown in Figure 28. (We neglect any further differences between instances

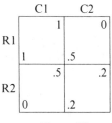

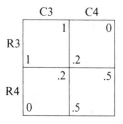

Figure 27   Figure 28

of a version.) S is trivial in one version but not in the other. Let R be the regularity of doing $R1$ or $C1$ (in the frequent version) or $R3$ or $C3$ (in the rare one). I take it that R ought not to qualify as a convention, since it is trivial in most instances of S. But it would qualify as a convention if we counted R' as its alternative, where R' is the regularity of doing $R1$ or $C1$ or $R4$ or $C4$. R' is an eligible regularity that is incompatible with R in some instances of S.

It would be better to require an alternative R' that is uniformly incompatible with R, incompatible for every agent in every instance of S. Now R in the example above is disqualified. Its only uniformly incompatible alternative would be R'', the regularity of doing $R2$ or

C2 or *R4* or *C4*. But *R''* is not an alternative to *R*, since *R''* usually fails to meet the requirement of conditional preference for conformity. In instances of the frequent version of *S*, no one wants to conform to *R''* even if his partner does.

If every instance of *S* is a coordination problem, and if uniform conformity to *R* is always a proper coordination equilibrium, then we can find another proper coordination equilibrium in every instance of *S*. Hence the regularity *R'* whereby one does his part of a selected second proper coordination equilibrium in every instance of *S* is an alternative to *R*, and *R* and *R'* are uniformly incompatible.

If we prefer, however, we do not have to require a uniformly incompatible alternative to *R*. As a (seemingly) weaker version, we could just require that for every instance of *S*, there is a suitable regularity *R'* which is incompatible with *R* (for everyone involved) in *that* instance. Partially incompatible alternatives to *R* are good enough if there are enough of them. The two versions are not really different. The strong version implies the weak version directly; and the weak version implies the strong version indirectly, since we can always get a uniformly incompatible alternative by patching together pieces of partially incompatible ones.

Therefore we might replace our original condition by two new ones. This one:

> In any instance of *S* among members of *P*, everyone has approximately the same preferences regarding all possible combinations of actions.

together with either this one (strong version):

> There is some possible regularity *R'* in the behavior of members of *P* in *S*, such that no one in any instance of *S* among members of *P* could conform both to *R'* and to *R*, and such that in any instance of *S* among members of *P*, everyone would prefer that everyone conform to *R'*, on condition that at least all but one conform to *R'*.

or this one (weak version):

> In any instance of S among members of P, there is some possible regularity R' in the behavior of members of P in S, such that no one in that instance of S could conform both to R' and to R, and such that everyone would prefer that everyone conform to R', on condition that at least all but one conform to R'.

I see nothing to choose between the two versions, and I choose the strong version for no good reason.

When S is a self-contained problem of interdependent decision, our new conditions agree with the original condition. But they do not require S to be self-contained. If not—as in my example of price setting, with S taken as a stretch of business activity long enough to include several pricing decisions—the new conditions are a natural extension of the original condition.

Let R be a convention regarding behavior in a coordination problem S; and let R' be another possible regularity, partially or uniformly incompatible with R, which would solve S. But suppose the coordination equilibrium we would reach by conforming to R' is much worse than the one we reach by conforming to R—so much worse, in fact, that it is only slightly preferred to some of the outcomes that are not coordination equilibria. Then do we really want to call R' a possible alternative convention? And do we want to say that R' contributes to the arbitrariness and conventionality of R? Perhaps not. Fortunately, our definition as it stands is likely to disqualify this R' as an alternative to R. It may be true that:

> In any instance of S among members of P, everyone would prefer that everyone conform to R', on condition that at least all but one conform to R'.

But it may not be true as an item of common knowledge. Our weak conditional preferences for conformity to R' may well fail to be indicated by any state of affairs A which we all believe to hold and which indicates to us that it holds. But of course we still require the satisfaction of the conditions to be common knowledge in P. And rightly: if our conditional preference for conformity to R' existed, but not as an item of common knowledge, R' could not have sustained itself in the way a convention does, so it is not true that R' could have been our convention instead of R.

Consider a convention establishing some meeting place. Its alternatives would be the possible regularities whereby we would meet at other places. Some places are better than others. Some are so bad we would forgo meeting rather than go there. Considering worse and worse places, we come to the point where conditional preference for conformity fails: some of us would not want to go to the place even if the others were there. Common knowledge of conditional preference fails sooner: there are places good enough that each would want to go there if the others were there, but not good enough that we could count on each other to want to go there if the others did, count on each other to count on each other to want to go there if the others did, and so on. These places do not provide alternatives to our convention, so they do not contribute to the conventionality of our meeting place.

Or consider the conventions of our language. Their alternatives are the conventions of other possible languages. But how about a hypothetical language—or shall we call it a cipher?—so clumsy that even after any amount of practice we would still take minutes of paper-and-pencil calculation to construct or construe its easiest sentences? All of us *might* find even that language better than none, worth learning to use among others who used it. But if it were not common knowledge that we would, this language would not be among the alternatives that make our actual language conventional.

If the only alternatives to R were of this deficient sort, R would not be a convention. Neither would it have been a convention under the original condition requiring that S be a coordination problem, since that would not have been common knowledge either. Nor should it be called a convention. If the alternatives to R are such an inconspicuous feature of the situation, R seems almost as trivial as if they were not there at all.

Can R' be an alternative to R if the idea of acting in conformity to R' has never occurred to anybody in P? The principle is the same: the unfamiliarity disqualifies R' if and only if it interferes with common knowledge of conditional preference for conformity to R'. It may or may not. Because the expectations and preferences mentioned in the definition of convention need only be general in *sensu diviso*, it does not matter if we have no general concept of action in conformity to R'. In fact, I argued in the last section that it would be all right if we had no general concept even of action in conformity to our actual convention. The unfamiliarity would matter, however, if it led one to fail to appreciate the advantage of some action in conformity to R' when presented with a particular instance of S in which the others did conform to R'; or if it led to a failure of common knowledge that one *would* appreciate that advantage.

Again there is no disagreement with the original condition, where it applies. If the only alternatives to R are disqualified by their unfamiliarity, it would not be common knowledge that S was a coordination problem. So R would not be a convention under either condition, though it might become one whenever the members of P became acquainted with the possibility of acting in conformity to R'.

What is not conventional among narrow-minded and inflexible people, who would not know what to do if others began to behave differently, may be conventional among more adaptable people. What is not conventional may become conventional when news arrives of aliens who behave differently; or when somebody invents a new way of behaving, even a new way no one adpots. When children and the feeble-minded conform to our conventions, they may not take part in them *as* conventions, for they may lack any conditional preference for conformity to an alternative; or they may have the proper preferences, but not as an item of common knowledge. I find these corollaries of our analysis of convention neither welcome nor unwelcome. The analysis is settling questions hitherto left open.

If it seems reasonable to exclude alternatives that are too unsatisfactory or unfamiliar, as not contributing to the arbitrariness of a convention, we have a new reason to require common knowledge. For it is by means of our common-knowledge requirement that we can exclude them without doing so *ad hoc*.

4. Degrees of Convention

We have confined our attention to perfect cases of convention, to which our definition applies without exceptions. But we cannot hope to find many perfect specimens in reality. It is time to be less strict, to allow for conventions that meet the present definition only for the most part or with high probability. Let us assemble the definition as amended so far:

A regularity R in the behavior of members of a population P when they are agents in a recurrent situation S is a *convention* if and only if it is true that, and it is common knowledge in P that, in any instance of S among members of P,

(1) everyone conforms to R;
(2) everyone expects everyone else to conform to R;
(3) everyone has approximately the same preferences regarding all possible combinations of actions;
(4) everyone prefers that everyone conform to R, on condition that at least all but one conform to R;
(5) everyone would prefer that everyone conform to R', on condition that at least all but one conform to R',

where R' is some possible regularity in the behavior of members of P in S, such that no one in any instance of S among members of P could conform both to R' and to R.

We can count many explicit and implicit universal quantifications; we want to find a reasonable way of relaxing some or all of these to almost-universal quantifications.

The common-knowledge requirement involves universal quantifications over P (see the definition of common knowledge). We need not allow any exception to these; anyone who might be called an exception might better be excluded from P. It follows, however, that most of our specifications of a population in which a convention holds will be only approximately correct.

There is no harm in allowing a few abnormal instances of S which violate some or all of clauses (1)–(5). So we replace "in any instance of S among members of P" by "in almost any instance of S among members of P." If we ever want more precision, we can replace it by "in a fraction of at least d_0 of all instances of S among member of P" with d_0 set slightly below one.

Nor is there any harm in allowing some, or even most, normal instances of S to contain a few abnormal agents who may be exceptions to the initial universal quantifications in some or all of clauses (1)-(5). So we replace each initial "everyone" by "almost everyone" or by "everyone in a fraction of at least d_i of all those involved," with each d_i set slightly below one. (We have d_1 for clause (1), d_2 for clause (2), d_3 for clause (3), and d_4 for clauses (4) and (5)—the same for both, since they are intended to be parallel.)

If we allow there to be a few agents who will not conform, we should allow the rest of the agents to know it; so "everyone else" in clause (2) should be replaced by "almost everyone else" or by "everyone else in a fraction of at least d_1 of all those involved." And if we allow the agents not to expect perfect conformity, we must not make their preferences for conformity conditional upon otherwise perfect conformity; otherwise we would not guarantee that they did prefer conformity in most cases. Their preferences should be such that if enough conform, then the more the better. (So one thing we do *not* tolerate is a convention to which most people want there to be exceptions, however few the exceptions they want.) Clause (4) should therefore be amended again to read "prefers that any one more conform to R, on condition that almost everyone conform to R" or "prefers that any one more conform to R, on condition that a fraction of at least d_1 of all those involved conform to R." Although this amendment makes clause (4) more strict rather than less, it is unavoidable given our relaxation of clauses (1) and (2). Clause (5) should be amended in the same way to keep it parallel to (4).

We may also tolerate a few exceptions to the required incompatibility between R and its alternative R'—exceptions for most agents in a few instances of S, for a few agents in most instances of S, or both. We replace the incompatibility clause by "such that almost no one in almost any instance of S among members of P could conform both to R' and to R," or by "such that for a fraction of at least d_5 of all pairs of an instance of S among members of P and an agent therein, the agent could not conform both to R' and to R," with d_5 set slightly below one.

Our final definition is therefore:

> A regularity R in the behavior of members of a population P when they are agents in a recurrent situation S is a *convention* if and only if it is true that, and it is common knowledge in P that, in almost any instance of S among members of P,
>
> (1) almost everyone conforms to R;
> (2) almost everyone expects almost everyone else to conform to R;
> (3) almost everyone has approximately the same preferences regarding all possible combinations of actions;
> (4) almost everyone prefers that any one more conform to R, on condition that almost everyone conform to R;
> (5) almost everyone would prefer that any one more conform to R', on condition that almost everyone conform to R',
>
> where R' is some possible regularity in the behavior of members of P in S, such that almost no one in almost any instance of S among members of P could conform both to R' and to R.

If anyone complains that our final definition of convention is imprecise, he is welcome to use the following quantitative definition.

> A regularity R in the behavior of members of a population P when they are agents in a recurrent situation S is a *convention*

to at least degrees d_0, d_1, d_2, d_3, d_4, d_5 if and only if it is true that, and it is common knowledge in P that, in a fraction of at least d_0 of all instances of S among members of P,

(1) everyone in a fraction of at least d_1 of all those involved conforms to R;

(2) everyone in a fraction of at least d_2 of all those involved expects everyone else in a fraction of at least d_1 of all those involved to conform to R;

(3) everyone in a fraction of at least d_3 of all those involved has approximately the same preferences regarding all possible combinations of actions;

(4) everyone in a fraction of at least d_4 of all those involved prefers that any one more conform to R, on condition that a fraction of at least d_1 of all those involved conform to R;

(5) everyone in a fraction of at least d_4 of all those involved would prefer that any one more conform to R', on condition that a fraction of at least d_1 of all those involved conform to R',

where R' is some possible regularity in the behavior of members of P in S, such that for a fraction of at least d_5 of all pairs of an instance of S among members of P and an agent involved therein, the agent could not conform both to R' and to R.

He may go on to define a convention as any regularity that is a convention to at least certain set degrees, which he may pick however he likes.

Let us define the *degree of conventionality* of a regularity R as the set of sextuples $\langle d_i \rangle$ such that R is a convention to at least degrees d_0, d_1, d_2, d_3, d_4, d_5. We can compare regularities with respect to their degrees of conventionality: R_1 is *more conventional* than R_2 if and only if the degree of conventionality of R_2 is a subset of the degree of conventionality of R_1. It would be interesting to find a single number that measures the degree of conventionality of a regularity; but all the ways I know to do this seem very artificial. If R is a convention according to the strict definition at the beginning of this section, then R is a convention to at least degrees 1, 1, 1, 1, 1, 1, and no other regularity can be more conventional.

5. Consequences of Conventions

Suppose R is a conventional regularity; and suppose R^* is some logical consequence of R. Is R^* therefore a convention in its own right?

There are trivial consequences of conventions, and we are not concerned with these. Let R be our convention of driving on the right; a logical consequence of R is that we drive on the surfaces of the roads, not ten feet in the air or ten feet underground. More trivially still, a tautology that is a consequence of anything is a consequence of any convention. What we want to consider are the consequences of conventions which *depend* on convention. Our consequence R^* depends on R only if there is a regularity R' that is an alternative to R (in the sense of section 3) and *not-R^** is a logical consequence of R'.

If so, R^* may be a convention. Suppose you and I want to meet every week; and suppose we spend alternate weeks in different towns $T1$ and $T2$. Town $T1$ has three acceptable meeting places: $P11$, $P12$, and $P13$. Town $T2$ also has three acceptable meeting places, each analogous to the like-numbered place in $T1$: $P21$, $P22$, and $P23$. Our convention R is this: in the weeks we spend in $T1$ we go to $P11$, and in the weeks we spend in $T2$ we go to $P21$. A consequence R^* of R is this: in the weeks we spend in $T1$ we go to $P11$. It is a dependent consequence, since *not-R^** would be a consequence of most of the alternatives to R. R^* is certainly a convention. In the situations to which R^* applies—our weeks in $T1$—it is common knowledge among us that we conform to R^*, we expect each other to conform to R^*, and uniform conformity to R^* is a coordination equilibrium in a coordination problem. In general, a specialization of a convention is a convention. Perhaps a consequence of a convention is a convention in its own right only if it is a specialization of the original convention.

Now let us look at a dependent consequence of a convention which is not itself a convention. Suppose there is just one town with three acceptable meeting places: *P1*, *P2*, and *P3*. Suppose we want to meet; but in case we fail to meet, it is desirable that one of us should go to *P3*. Suppose our payoff matrix is as given in Figure 29, and suppose

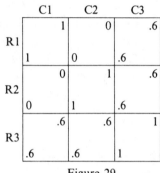

	C1	C2	C3
R1	1 / 1	0 / 0	.6 / .6
R2	0 / 0	1 / 1	.6 / .6
R3	.6 / .6	.6 / .6	1 / 1

Figure 29

our convention *R* is to go to *P1*. Let *R** be the regularity of going either to *P1* or to *P2*. *R** is a consequence of *R*; and it is a dependent consequence, since *not-R** would follow from the regularity of going to *P3*, which is an alternative to *R*. We conform to *R** and expect each other to, and both of these facts are common knowledge between us. But *R** is not a convention because, I contend, it is not the case that each of us prefers to conform to *R** conditionally upon the other's conforming to *R**. Given only that you will conform to *R**, with no indication of whether you will do so by going to *P1* or by going to *P2*, I prefer to violate *R** by going to *P3*. The same is true for you with respect to me.

The case is not entirely clear, however. Consider that what we call a preference conditional upon some state of affairs *A* is almost always conditional also upon some background state of affairs *B*, which we regard as a fixed part of the environment. To say that I prefer to drive on the right if others do is really to say that I prefer to drive on the right if others do *and* if various familiar facts about the causes and effects of collisions continue to hold. Now it is a fact, and common knowledge between us, that if either of us conforms to R^*, he will do so by conforming to R; in other words, it is a fact and common knowledge that we will not go to $P2$. If this fact were included in the fixed background, then each of us *would* prefer to conform to R^*, conditionally upon the other's conforming to R^* and upon background. I am sure it is wrong to include in the fixed background this fact, that if either of us conforms to R^* it will be by conforming to R. But I have no theory to explain why it is wrong. Roughly, the reason is this: in considering preferences for actions conditionally upon actions, the background ought to be kept neutral as to whether actions of the general sort under consideration are done or not.

III | Convention Contrasted

1. Agreement

In Chapter I.3 we saw how agents involved in a single, unrepeated coordination problem might do well to achieve coordination by agreeing explicitly that each is to do his part of a certain coordination equilibrium. But I stated, too, that explicit agreement was not the only means of coordination.

Similarly, our explicit agreement to conform to some suitable regularity R is a means—a good means, but not the only one—of arranging once and for all to achieve coordination whenever a certain recurrent coordination problem S arises among us. In agreeing face to face to conform to R, each of us is manifesting his (pre-existing or newly formed) propensity to conform to R; and he is doing so under circumstances in which it is common knowledge among us that all of us are watching him. Consequently it becomes common knowledge that all of us are likely to conform to R. Since it is also common knowledge that each prefers to conform to R conditionally upon conformity by others involved with him in S,[1] each has all the more reason and propensity to conform—and this, too, is common knowledge. Common knowledge of a propensity to conform produces conforming action when S next arises; conforming action renews our common knowledge of a propensity to conform. A convention is under way.

Our convention is the product of our agreement and so—in a

[1] If it was not before, it becomes common knowledge during the discussion before we agree, as each of us manifests his conditional preference for conforming.

83

way—are all our conforming actions forevermore. But to say we act as we do because we once agreed to would be badly misleading. It suggests that our agreement continues to influence our actions directly, just as it did at first; actually its major effect is transmitted through a growing causal chain of expectations, actions, expectations, actions, and so on. The direct influence fades away in days, years, or lifetimes. We forget our agreement. We cease to feel bound by old promises (if our agreement *was* an exchange of promises; as we saw in the case of a single coordination problem, an exchange of manifestations of present intent is apt to be good enough). We leave the population, and are replaced by heirs who were not party to the agreement. But the indirect influence of the agreement is constantly renewed, and in time it comes to predominate. Then a convention created by agreement is no longer different from one created otherwise: it bears no trace of its origin.

In fact, a convention begun by agreement may not become a convention, on my definition, until the direct influence of the agreement has had time to fade. This depends on the nature of the agreement. Suppose we all swore a solemn and public oath to conform to R come what may. Then for a while we might all prefer *un*conditionally to conform to R, each determined that even were the others to break their oaths and conform to some alternative regularity R', still he would rather keep his oath. Even if our preferences for conforming to R were in fact conditional upon conformity by others, it might not be common knowledge that they were. For the onus of oath breaking might create uncertainty, be expected to create uncertainty, and so on. We have a convention only after the force of our promises has faded to the point where it is both true and common knowledge that each would conform to some alternative regularity R' instead of R if the others did.

If, on the other hand, we agreed by exchanging conditional promises binding us to conform to R only if others did, or by exchanging noncommittal declarations of intent, the resulting regularity would be a perfectly good convention at once.

To see how a convention might start by an agreement or otherwise, let us take as our example a convention that does not yet exist: a convention among logicians establishing a standard notation. There is no such convention now. Since many notations are in use, everyone feels free to indulge his preference. But such a convention could exist. If any of today's notations were used as uniformly as standard arithmetical notation, everyone would use it. No one would insist on using his favorite notation if another notation were standard. (An eccentric notation would be more troublesome for readers used to a standard notation than it is for readers used to our present chaos.)

Imagine that the diversity of notations becomes more troublesome than it is now. Every author invents his own notation; some adopt it, some learn it but do not use it by choice, and others cannot even read it. Then the Association for Symbolic Logic might hold a meeting at which the problem is discussed; everyone present expresses the hope that a standard notation will be established; and *Principia* notation is elected by a vote of the meeting. If so, those who attended the meeting would consider themselves, and each other, to have expressed an intent to use *Principia* notation henceforth if most other logicians do too. Their exchange of declarations of intent in a face-to-face meeting would be an agreement sufficient to start a convention.

But the same convention might begin in other ways instead. Imagine some of the possibilities.

A few prominent logicians—say, the editors of the *Journal of Symbolic Logic*—might publish in the *JSL* a joint statement that the troublesome diversity of notation ought to be remedied, and that, in their opinion, *Principia* notation ought to be used exclusively henceforth. Since it is common knowledge among logicians that they all read the *JSL*, it would become common knowledge among logicians that most logicians had read the statement. And if it was common knowledge among logicians that most logicians would be inclined to follow such a suggestion if others did, then it would be common knowledge that most logicians would have a much increased propensity to use *Principia* notation. Given a sufficient interest in conforming to any standard, a convention to use *Principia* notation might result.

In this case only a few people play an active part in initiating the new convention; the rest are a responsive audience.

Or there might be no attempt to create a new convention. Several logicians, disturbed by the proliferation of notations and concerned for the intelligibility of their work, might decide independently to switch from their favorite notations to whichever notation seemed to be best known, namely, *Principia*. The resulting increase in use of *Principia* notation might seem like the beginning of a trend, so others would be inclined to switch and to expect each other to switch. Again the result would be a convention.

Or there might be a spate of works in *Principia* notation for no particular reason at all. Just by coincidence, many of the logicians who prefer *Principia* notation might happen to publish at once. An ostensible trend is created all the same, which others may follow.

In short, certain conditions—common knowledge of a general preference for using any sufficiently popular notation, plus common knowledge that logicians can tell how much the various notations are being used—tend somewhat to amplify any fluctuation in the logicians' expectations and propensities about their choice of notation. A convention is produced when a big enough fluctuation meets strong enough amplifying forces. The source of the fluctuation is unimportant, given its size. It does not matter whether it was created with the intention of starting a convention or whether it occurred in some or all of the population.

Granting that explicit agreement is only one of several possible origins for conventions, we may still wonder whether it enjoys some special status. Is it true, perhaps, that all conventions *could* originate by agreement? I offer three counterarguments.

First, recall the example of Hume's rowers, a conventional regularity we cannot describe. We cannot describe it in practice; if we could in principle, it would be by using more time and more measuring instruments than the rowers could have at their disposal. But this argument only goes to show that their convention could not originate by an agreement that is a purely verbal exchange. They can perfectly well agree to row *thus*, specifying a rhythm of rowing by demonstrating it.

Next, suppose a convention produces coordination to serve some purpose that would be defeated somehow by the very act of agreeing. Then that convention could not originate by agreement, for an agreement would destroy the point of conforming to the convention. Take two people who find it expedient to keep up a facade of hostility (say, leaders of rival political parties). They could use a convention specifying what sort of opinions they are to profess on any topic, lest they find themselves in public agreement—to the embarrassment of both. But they cannot create a convention by agreeing. For that would destroy their facade by confessing their common interest in preserving it, leaving them nothing to coordinate for. (It is true that they might agree in secret. But secrecy would not help them if—to change the example—we suppose that their facade is one they present primarily *to themselves*. If so, however, the counterexample is suspect because the agents are deceiving themselves. They believe in their facade while taking precautions to avoid encountering the evidence that would disillusion them. So they cannot safely be treated as rational agents with coherent beliefs.)

Last, consider this argument, given by Quine and others.[2] The first convention of language to be established could not originate by an agreement conducted in a convention-governed language. So even if *any* convention of language could originate by such agreement, not *all* of them could. (Thus this argument differs from the two above, which purported to show that particular conventions could not originate by agreement.) I offer this rejoinder: an agreement sufficient to create a convention need not be a transaction involving language or any other conventional activity. All it takes is an exchange of

[2] By Quine in "Truth by Convention"; by Bertrand Russell in *The Analysis of Mind* (London: Allen and Unwin, 1921), p. 190; by William Alston in *Philosophy of Language* (Englewood Cliffs, New Jersey: Prentice-Hall, 1964), p. 57. All three take it to be an argument that there are no conventions of language, since they believe that conventions properly so-called must be created by agreement.

manifestations of a propensity to conform to a regularity. These manifestations might simply be displays of conforming action in various appropriate situations, done during a face-to-face meeting in order to create a convention. Such an exchange of displays might be called an "agreement" without stretching the term too far.

I take it that all three arguments are inconclusive. Construing "agreement" generously, maybe all conventions could, in principle, originate by agreements. What is clear is that they need not. And often they do not: Chapter I.5 should suggest familiar examples of conventions originating otherwise. Conventions are like fires: under favorable conditions, a sufficient concentration of heat spreads and perpetuates itself. The nature of the fire does not depend on the original source of heat. Matches may be our best fire starters, but that is no reason to think of fires started otherwise as any the less fires.

2. Social Contracts

It seems (subject to weak objections) that a convention is a regularity in behavior which holds *as if* in consequence of an agreement so to behave, by virtue of a general preference for general conformity to that regularity. Now this is just how one might describe a social contract, given the sophistication to treat the original making of the contract as a fictitious dramatization of our present reasons for conforming. Is my concept of convention nothing but our familiar concept of social contract, as inherited from Hobbes, Locke, and Rousseau, demythologized and applied to matters other than political allegiance and social solidarity?

It is not. The concept of social contract, as I understand it, is different in principle from that of convention (though there are descriptions, like the one above, crude enough to miss the difference). Nor do the extensions of these concepts coincide, though they overlap heavily.

I propose to define a *social contract* roughly as any regularity R

in the behavior of members of a population P when they are agents in a situation S, such that it is true, and common knowledge in P, that:

Any member of P who is involved in S acts in conformity to R.

Each member of P prefers the state of general conformity to R (by members of P in S) to a certain contextually definite state of general nonconformity to R, called the *state of nature* relative to social contract R.

The state of nature is not just any state of general nonconformity to R (by members of P in S); it is somehow distinguished.[3] The state of nature relative to Hobbes's social contract (whereby we constitute a leviathan by regular obedience to a sovereign) is understood to be anarchy and the war of all against all. It is not peaceful anarchy and not the existence of a leviathan under some other sovereign, although these would also be states of general nonconformity to our actual social contract. Peaceful anarchy does not qualify because Hobbes believes it to be unstable; the existence of a leviathan under some other sovereign does not qualify because it is too similar in kind to the social contract in question.

The state of nature relative to R is a state of general nonconformity to R; a state of general nonconformity to other regularities similar in kind to R; and a state in which no one is relying very heavily on any anticipated regularity in others' action. No one stands to lose too much if his expectations about his neighbors prove wrong. This is an especially stable state. And it is a state we might fall into if somehow we had to start from scratch with no strong mutual expectations (hence the *a priori* plausibility of the myth that primitive peoples live in a state of nature).

[3] See R. P. Wolff, "A Refutation of Rawls' Theorem on Justice," *Journal of Philosophy,* 63 (1966), pp. 179–190. Wolff, replying to the ideal contractualism proposed by John Rawls in "Justice as Fairness," *Philosophical Review,* 67 (1958), pp. 164–194, objects that Rawls has given us no way to identify the "baseline"—that is, the state of nature—with which a social contract should be compared.

Observe that because the state of nature relative to R is possible, it follows that members of P do not prefer unconditionally to conform to R—which, had it not been implied, should have been stated in the definition of social contract.

My definition of social contract paralleled that of convention as far as possible in order to show the location of difference: in the nature of the general preference for general conformity. Preferring something is preferring it *to* something else, and the second term of the preference is not the same. For convention, we require that each agent prefer general conformity to conformity by all but himself, ignoring his preferences regarding states of general nonconformity. For social contract, we require that each agent prefer general conformity to a certain state of general nonconformity, ignoring his preferences regarding conformity by all but himself.

Consider the regularity R of obeying a sovereign. Let us see how R might be a convention, a social contract, both, or neither. Suppose the status quo is this: we almost always obey the sovereign's commands:

(1) to refrain from taking one another's goods;
(2) To hand over all we can spare to support the sovereign in luxury;
(3) to help catch and punish anyone who breaks any of these three commands.

(If anyone is offended by this caricature of political society, let him turn it into an example about castaways, gangsters, or nations.) Each of us has some preference ranking of the following three states, each with its own advantages and disadvantages:

(SQ) The status quo. I am protected from my neighbors by the sovereign's power to enforce his first command. I am safe from the sovereign's police power because I do not try to disobey. But I am poor because I help to support the sovereign and I do not take others' goods.

(SN) The state of nature. Nobody commands general obedience, so I have no organized police power to fear. I do not help to support a sovereign, for we have none. But I must work to protect my goods from my neighbors, and I live in fear that I will fail.

(*LD*) Lone disobedience. My goods are protected from my neighbors. I can get rich because sometimes I take my neighbors' goods and I do not contribute my full share toward the sovereign's support. But I live in fear that the sovereign, with my neighbors' help, will catch and punish me.

Ignoring indifference, each of us must have one of the six possible preference rankings, not necessarily the same for everyone:

SN	*SQ*	*SQ*	*LD*	*SN*	*LD*
SQ	*LD*	*SN*	*SQ*	*LD*	*SN*
LD	*SN*	*LD*	*SN*	*SQ*	*SQ*

(writing the most preferred state at the top, the least preferred one at the bottom). One's preferences will depend on his temperament; on his opinion of the character of his neighbors and of the sovereign; on his estimate of the likelihood that others would imitate his disobedience; on his estimate of his ability to make a living, to defend himself in the state of nature, or to escape punishment for disobedience; and on the values he assigns to security, wealth, relief from the task of self-defense, the welfare of his neighbors, the welfare of the sovereign, justice, peace, and trust.

If *R* is a convention, the only preference rankings that occur among us (except in a negligible minority) are the three in which *SQ* is ranked above *LD* so that each prefers to conform to *R* conditionally upon the others' conformity:

SN	*SQ*	*SQ*
SQ	*LD*	*SN*
LD	*SN*	*LD*

It makes no difference where *SN* occurs in anyone's ranking.

If *R* is a social contract, the only rankings that occur among us (except in a negligible minority) are the three in which SQ is ranked above SN so that each is benefiting from the general conformity to R:

SQ	SQ	LD
LD	SN	SQ
SN	LD	SN

It makes no difference where LD occurs in anyone's ranking.

If R is both a social contract and a convention, the only rankings that occur among us (except in a negligible minority) are the two in which SQ is preferred to both alternatives:

SQ	SQ
LD	SN
SN	LD

If R is a convention but not a social contract, some or all of us have the preference ranking:

$$SN$$
$$SQ$$
$$LD$$

These people are trapped. They want the convention abandoned. But nobody dares to do his part of abandoning it unless he can count on many others to abandon it along with him. To take the extreme case: if *all* of us prefer the state of nature to the status quo, the convention owes its survival entirely to the difficulty of organizing *concerted* disobedience to the sovereign's commands. (If the sovereign values his position, he would do well to issue a fourth command prohibiting any efforts at such organization.) All conventions are metastable, but this one is apt to be less stable than most, since we have an incentive to get together to change it if we can. The convention not to admit that the emperor had no clothes was not a social contract. Everyone wanted to break it, but only the little boy dared to break it *alone*. When he did, the convention collapsed and the state of nature was restored.

If R is a social contract but not a convention, some or all of us have the preference ranking:

$$LD$$
$$SQ$$
$$SN$$

We may well ask why these people continue to conform. For in passing up opportunities to gain by disobeying the sovereign's commands, they must be acting against their own preferences.

If we think of someone's preferences as the resultant of *all* the more or less enduring forces that go into determining his choices, then action that regularly goes against preference is barely possible. It would have to be due to transient forces, and different ones on different occasions. And it is hard to see how it could become common knowledge that people would regularly act against preference, since action against preference is inherently exceptional. So on this, our most common, concept of preference, it is almost impossible for a social contract not to be a convention because some prefer not to conform although others do.

Sometimes, however, we think of preference more narrowly as the resultant of choice-determining forces *other than* a sense of duty. Our accepted moral obligations can and do regularly override our preferences in this narrow sense. So we could say of a man that his preferences are

$$LD$$
$$SQ$$
$$SN$$

but that he obeys the sovereign's commands against his own preferences because he considers himself to be under a moral obligation to do so. He might believe with Locke that he gave his fellowmen a tacit promise to obey if they obeyed, when he first passed up an opportunity to leave the country; or he might believe with John Rawls that he is under an obligation of fair play to reciprocate the benefits he has willingly received through the others' obedience.[4] Either way, his obligation arises because he prefers the status quo to the state of nature. Hence, for any social contract, the conditions of such obligations are present for everyone. If everyone will recognize such obligations, everyone will honor the social contract whether or not he prefers to. The social contract will persist, and it may be common knowledge that it will. But it is not a convention, not if the preferences mentioned in the definition of convention are taken as preferences in the narrow sense.

If we return to our ordinary, wider concept of preference, it remains true that many social contracts will be sustained by the moral obligations of tacit consent or fair play, as recognized by the agents involved. But these accepted obligations will be counted as a component of preferences, not as an independent choice-determining force. Since we accept these obligations, our preference rankings will be

$$\begin{array}{ccc} SQ & & SQ \\ LD & or & SN \\ SN & & LD \end{array}$$

instead of

$$\begin{array}{c} LD \\ SQ \\ SN \end{array}$$

as they might be (for some of us) otherwise. So our social contract is a convention after all. But it is a convention because of the modification of our preferences by obligations, and these obligations exist because it is a social contract.

Thus the possibility of a social contract that is not a convention

---

[4] But the content of our illustrative social contract is not the content either Locke or Rawls had in mind; rather it is the simple and desperate contract of Hobbes's *Leviathan*. I see no reason why men should not adhere to Hobbes's contract for Locke's or Rawls's reasons.

(in the way so far considered) is problematic; it depends on adopting the less common of our two concepts of preference, that in which preference is opposed to obligation.

There is a quite different way, less problematic, for a social contract not to be a convention. Recall that we required a convention to be one of several alternative conventions, whereas a social contract need have no other alternative than the state of nature. The state of nature need not be a state in which we achieve coordination equilibria conforming to a regularity. Certainly Hobbes's state of nature is not: battles in the war of all against all do not result in equilibria (since the loser will wish he had adopted a different strategy), let alone coordination equilibria.[5] So a social contract may fail to be a convention for lack of an alternative, even though it is a regularity whereby we reach coordination equilibria and everyone therefore prefers to conform to it if the others do.

If we recurrently find ourselves involved in a certain situation (not a coordination problem) represented by the payoff matrix in Figure 30, and all of us regularly act so as to achieve the coordination

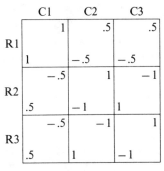

Figure 30

[5] In Rousseau's example of the stag hunt, on the other hand, the state of nature relative to the social contract of all helping to hunt the stag together is the state in which we all catch rabbits by ourselves; and this state of nature *is* a state in which we reach coordination equilibria.

equilibrium $\langle R1, C1 \rangle$, our regularity is a social contract, and it is a regularity whereby we achieve coordination equilibria, but it is not a convention. For there is only one other stable state, the state of nature: that in which we choose at random every time between $R2$ and $R3$ (or $C2$ and $C3$). And the outcomes we reach in the state of nature—$\langle R2, C2 \rangle$, $\langle R2, C3 \rangle$, $\langle R3, C2 \rangle$, and $\langle R3, C3 \rangle$—are not coordination equilibria, indeed not equilibria at all. (We do achieve an equilibrium combination of *mixed* strategies, but that is an equilibrium only in an extended sense and still is not a coordination equilibrium.) So the state of nature is not a convention, and our regularity of choosing $R1$ and $C1$ cannot be a convention either.

As an example, suppose that every Friday the same ten of us go to a Chinese restaurant where we are served, among other things, a plate of twenty fried shrimp. We would like three or four each, but for the sake of good relations each is willing to limit himself to two if and only if everyone else limits himself too. No one cares to restrain himself unless he can be sure that thereby he allows everyone to get his share. So there are two stable states: a social contract, whereby everyone takes two, or the state of nature, a scramble in which the first comers take all they want until none are left. The state of nature is not a state in which we achieve coordination equilibria, so the social contract is not a convention, although each prefers to conform to it if the others do. And that is as it should be: this social contract does seem to lack the characteristic arbitrariness of a convention.

Finally, a social contract might fail to be a convention, or vice versa, in still another way: the items of common knowledge required in the definition of convention are not the same as those required in the definition of social contract. So a suitable lack of common knowledge might disqualify a regularity as a convention but not as a social contract, or vice versa. It is hard to see how such a discriminating lack of common knowledge could occur; generally, the conditions that make for common knowledge of any of the facts of a case make for common knowledge of all of them.

3. Norms

The definition I gave of convention did not contain normative terms: "ought," "should," "good," and others. Nor have we reason to expect normative terms to occur essentially in any equivalent definition. So "convention" itself, on my analysis, is not a normative term.

Nevertheless, conventions may *be* a species of norms: regularities to which we believe one ought to conform. I shall argue that they are. There are certain probable consequences implied by the fact that an action would conform to a convention (whatever the action and whatever the convention) which are presumptive reasons, according to our common opinions, why that action ought to be done.

Suppose R is a convention in population P regarding behavior in situation S. And suppose I am a member of population P in situation S. Then by the definition of convention, and without regard to what R, P, and S may be, this supposition makes it probable that:

(1) Most other members of P involved with me in situation S will conform to R.

(2) I prefer that, if most other members of P involved with me in S will conform, then I conform also.

(3) Most other members of P involved with me in S expect, with reason, that I will conform.

(4) Most other members of P involved with me in S prefer that, if most of them conform, I conform also.

(5) I have reason to believe that (1)–(4) hold.

Had we supposed R to be a convention to degrees 1, 1, 1, 1, 1, 1, then that and the supposition that I am a member of P in S would have implied (1)–(5), even strengthened by putting "all" for "most" throughout. But, since we chose to allow for conventions that are less than perfectly conventional, we must hedge by stating (1)–(5) to allow exceptions and by allowing exceptions to (1)–(5) themselves. But (1)–(5) must hold in *most* cases in which people decide whether to conform to any convention. Thus in any given case—barring evidence that the case is exceptional—each of (1)-(5) probably holds: so probably (although less probably) all of them hold.

And if they all do hold in any case, then so do these:

(6) I have reason to believe that my conforming would answer to my own preferences.
(7) I have reason to believe that my conforming would answer to the preferences of most other members of P involved with me in S; and that they have reason to expect me to conform.

And (6) and (7), when true, are presumptive reasons why I ought to conform. For we do presume, other things being equal, that one ought to do what answers to his own preferences. And we presume, other things being equal, that one ought to do what answers to others' preferences, especially when they may reasonably expect one to do so. For any action conforming to any convention, then, we would recognize these two (probable and presumptive) reasons why it ought to be done. We would not, so far as I can tell, recognize any similarly general reasons why it ought not to be done. This is what I mean by calling conventions a species of norms.

Of course, for any particular action conforming to a convention, there may be all sorts of other reasons why it ought or ought not to be done. (There might also be reasons to believe that the case is an exceptional one in which [6] or [7] does not hold.) The convention in question might be one that was adopted by an exchange of promises, so that a conforming action ought to be done to keep one's promise. Or it might be a convention that is also a social contract, so that a conforming action ought to be done to reciprocate the benefit one derives from conformity by others. On the other hand, it might be an understanding between oligopolists to fix prices or between pickpockets to work in a team, so that a conforming action ought not to be done since it is not in the public interest. As always, the various presumptive reasons why an action ought or ought not to be done are balanced off against each other; (6) and (7) might easily be outweighed. Their importance is not that they are especially weighty considerations. Rather, it is that they are especially general: for any convention whatever, they must enter into deliberations about whether to conform to it.

Any convention is, by definition, a norm which there is some presumption that one ought to conform to. I shall now argue that it is also, by definition, a socially enforced norm: one is expected to conform, and failure to conform tends to evoke unfavorable responses from others. For if R is a convention in population P regarding behavior in situation S, and I am a member of P in S, then (by the definition of convention, and no matter what R, P, and S may be) probably:

> (8) Most other members of P involved with me in S expect me to conform.
> (9) Most other members of P involved with me in S have reason to believe that conditions (1)–(5) hold.

And whenever (9) holds, so do these:

> (10) Most members of P involved with me in S have reason to believe that my conforming would answer to my own preferences.
> (11) Most members of P involved with me in S have reason to believe that I have reason to believe both that my conforming would answer to their preferences and that they have reason to expect me to conform.

So if they see me fail to conform, not only have I gone against their expectations; they will probably be in a position to infer that I have knowingly acted contrary to my own preferences, and contrary to their preferences and their reasonable expectations. They will be surprised, and they will tend to explain my conduct discreditably. The poor opinions they form of me, and their reproaches, punishment, and distrust are the unfavorable responses I have evoked by my failure to conform to the convention.

Consider our example of a convention that the original caller calls back and the called party waits when a telephone call is cut off. Suppose I fail to conform—I wait when I am the original caller or I call back when I am the called party. My partner knows what I did. He knows that I should have known that by acting as I did I would fail to restore our connection. He may guess that I acted without thinking; or that I was too dull ever to learn the convention; or that I was bored with talking to him anyway and did not want the call restored; or that I expected *him* to be at fault in one of these ways and violated the convention to counteract the violation I expected from him. Whatever he thinks, his opinion of me suffers. So does the way he is likely to treat me in the future. These are bad consequences, and my interest in avoiding them strengthens my conditional preference for conforming.

4. Rules

We would certainly call many conventions rules. For instance, those presented in Chapter I.5 as established solutions to the eleven sample coordination problems might all naturally be called rules—though probably with a qualification: "tacit" rules, "informal" rules, "unwritten" rules, or the like. But certainly not all so-called rules are conventions. Let us consider several kinds of counterexamples.

Sometimes mere generalizations, laws of nature, or even mathematical truths are called rules. These rules may have nothing to do with the conduct of human agents, except that human agents might benefit by taking account of them. For instance, we have this passage in a cookbook:

> Here is a cardinal rule that has very few exceptions: *All* meat is more tender and juicy if cooked at *low* instead of high temperature.[6]

[6] B. B. McLean and T. W. Campbell, *The Meat and Poultry Cookbook* (New York: Pocket Books, 1960), p. 19.

And this theorem that an algebra text calls "Descartes' Rule of Signs":

> An equation $f(x) = 0$ cannot have more positive roots than there are changes of sign in $f(x)$, and cannot have more negative roots than there are changes of sign in $f(-x)$.[7]

Other so-called rules are strategic maxims, hypothetical imperatives stating what a human agent might do to gain some end. These rules state generalizations regarding the tendency of certain actions to accomplish certain ends. We are given these "general rules for using any insecticide":

> Treat any household insecticide, no matter how labeled, as a poison. Never use insecticides on nursery walls, playpens, cribs, toys, or places where infants creep. Buy insecticides only as needed. Store them in a locked cabinet. Once insects are conquered, bury all leftover insecticides deep in the trash container.[8]

And this "rule for reducing a recurring decimal to a vulgar fraction" (a hypothetical imperative based on a theorem):

> For the numerator subtract the integral number consisting of the non-recurring figures from the integral number consisting of the non-recurring and recurring figures; for the denominator take a number consisting of as many nines as there are recurring figures followed by as many ciphers as there are non-recurring figures.[9]

Here are rules for cultivating taste:

> the first rule for the student of wine is to trust his own palate—to believe in its physical ability to record as many sensations as anybody else's . . . The second important rule for the student

[7] H. S. Hall and S. R. Knight, *Higher Algebra* (London: Macmillan, 1960), p. 459.
[8] *Consumer Reports,* 30 (1965), no. 12, p. 156.
[9] Hall and Knight, *Higher Algebra,* p. 43.

is that he must have the courage to change his mind. As experience grows and perception becomes keener, his taste is certain to change and wines which at first pleased may now bore or actively displease.[10]

Other rules are hypothetical imperatives reinforced by authoritative codification and enforced by sanctions. This rule might appear on a poster in a chemical plant:

Employees are not to smoke within 100 yards of any acetone vat; violation will be considered ground for immediate dismissal.

Not to smoke near an acetone vat already answers to any worker's interest in avoiding fires, regardless of whether or not his fellow workers smoke near acetone vats and regardless of whether management has laid down a rule against it. The official rule reminds employees of this hypothetical imperative. It also notifies them of the fact that it is management's policy to fire anyone caught smoking near an acetone vat; it is a threat or warning[11] designed to deter them further from doing so.

Other rules are threats or warnings issued by some authority or power to control the behavior of a class of people against their own preferences. A POW camp might have a rule that prisoners are not to gather in groups of more than six, violation to be punished by ten days on bread and water. A local protection mob might make a rule that lunch counters are to rent one pinball machine for every ten seats, violation to be punished by arson. Since one's incentive to obey is the same whether or not the rest obey (unless mass disobedience would destroy the enforcer's will or power to punish), a rule of this kind is not a convention.

[10] Allan Sichel, *The Penguin Book of Wines* (Baltimore: Penguin Books, 1965), p. 22.

[11] Most likely a warning. The distinction is Schelling's; see *Strategy of Conflict*, pp. 123–124. A *warning* is a statement that if you do *A* which I don't like, you probably will thereby give me a good reason to do *B* which you don't like. A *threat* is a declaration of my present intent to do *B* if you do *A*, whether or not I would then have any good reason to do *B*.

It might, however, be conventional in the sense that it forms the *content* of a convention among the rule makers. Suppose the commandant of a POW camp who is exceptionally strict or lenient will get into trouble. Then all the commandants have an interest in adopting the same schedule of penalties. If so, it might be a convention among the commandants that the penalty for gathering in groups of more than six is to be ten days on bread and water. The rules assigning that penalty in the several camps are, in a sense, conventional; but they are not conventions.

Other rules codify regularities of the kinds discussed in section 2 as social contracts that are not conventions. If we adopt the narrow concept of preference in which one's preferences do not include his acceptance of moral obligations—for example, obligations of tacit consent or fair play—this class of rules is a large one. These rules prescribe behavior for each agent which may go against his own preferences (in the narrow sense) but which answers to the preferences of everyone else concerned. They are hypothetical imperatives stating what one should do to keep tacit promises, what one should do to reciprocate benefits, and so on. They may also carry threats or warnings that violation will incur specified (institutionalized or informal) sanctions. Criminal law may consist largely of rules of this sort, at least in a traditional society without legislation. So may part of our social morality, for instance the rule that one should keep his promises. So may a library's regulations regarding the return of borrowed books.

Finally, there can be rules that are not conventions only because they are enforced with sanctions so strong that one would have a decisive reason to obey even if others did not. Take the convention whereby logicians might establish a standard notation; and suppose that after the convention had existed for twenty years, any editor would reject out of hand a manuscript using nonstandard notation. The editors would then have made a rule requiring standard notation, a rule enforced by the sanction of nonpublication. But it is no longer a convention, since each logician has a decisive reason to use standard notation whether his colleagues do or not. He still wants to use whatever notation his colleagues use, and he would like to follow them if they all switched; but he would not be likely to care enough to forgo publication. (I assume some inertia on the part of the editors, so that they might try to insist on the old standard notation for a time, even after most logicians had switched to a new notation. If the editors too would switch immediately, their enforcement of standard notation does not detract from its conventionality.) Under these conditions, it is not true of any nonstandard notation that everyone would prefer to use it if the others did; therefore the use of standard notation is no longer a convention.

Perhaps there are other kinds of so-called rules that are not conventions, but this completes my list.

It is harder to argue that some conventions are not naturally called rules. (Indeed, it is hard to show that there is *any* regularity that could not be called a rule in *some* context.) But consider conventions that coexist and contrast with rules that are rules par excellence, say in a game. The game of Jotto is definable as activity conforming to the following rules.

> There are two players.
> Each chooses a five-letter word for the other to guess.
> Each in turn proposes a five-letter test word of his choice, and the other tells him how many letters his word has in common with the word he is guessing.
> When a player proposes the word the other chose for him to guess, he wins.

These are perfect specimens of rules. They define the game of Jotto. They are easily codified, as above, and their codifications are used in teaching people to play Jotto. Their violation would be taken as decisive evidence of inability or unwillingness to play Jotto. They are conventional; but they are not the only conventions in the game. Any group of players will develop understandings—tacit, local, temporary, informal conventions—to settle questions left open by the listed rules. What foreign words, slang, proper names, acronyms, or coinages are admissible words? May a player have an earlier answer repeated (without wasting his turn) if he thinks a mistake was made? And so on. We might call these understandings rules—unwritten rules, informal rules—if we like; but we would also be inclined to emphasize their differences from the listed rules by saying that they are not rules, but only conventions.

I hope my examples have left an impression that the class of so-called rules is a miscellany, with many debatable members. We might be tempted to try distinguishing several senses of the word "rule," hoping that one of them would agree with my definition of convention. I doubt that the project would succeed. Many senses could be proposed, but probably they would turn out not to be distinct enough to merit the name of different senses. We seem to be dealing with an especially messy cluster concept, and one in which the relative importance of different conditions varies with the subject matter, with the contrasts one wants to make, and with one's philosophical preconceptions. (It should be clear now why I have been contrasting conventions not with rules but with "so-called rules." I wanted to recognize the variation in what we would call a rule without saying whether this variation is ambiguity, boundary vagueness, or what.)

William Alston—speaking, I think, for many philosophers—has made the following proposal.

> Like the social contract theory in political science, the idea that words get their meaning by convention is a myth if taken literally. But like the social contract theory, it may be an embodiment, in mythical form, of important truths that could be stated in more sober terms. It is our position that this truth is best stated in terms of the notions of rules. That is, what really demarcates symbols is the fact that they have what meaning they have by virtue of the fact that for each there are rules in force, in some community, that govern their use . . . Henceforth, we shall feel free to use the term "conventional" purged of misleading associations, as shorthand for "on the basis of rules."[12]

[12] *Philosophy of Language,* pp. 57–58.

But if my analysis of convention is sound, and if the class of so-called rules is as miscellaneous as my examples seem to show, then it would be better to do exactly the opposite: to understand the "rules of language" we encounter in the works of philosophers of language as tacit conventions. We have no excuse for being misled by the misleading association of convention with explicit agreement.

Nor shall we be misled by misleading associations of the word "rule." When someone says that language is governed by rules, we are likely to think of rules that have been codified by some authority, or easily could be; of rules that are enforced by sanctions, formal or informal; of rules that are mentioned in teaching or criticizing the use of language. Paul Ziff, for one, has been misled into skepticism by just these misleading associations, as we see from his denunciation of rules of language:

> I am concerned with regularities: I am not concerned with rules. Rules have virtually nothing to do with speaking or understanding a natural language.
>
> Philosophers are apt to have the following picture of language. Speaking a language is a matter of engaging in a certain activity, an activity in accordance with certain rules. If the rules of the language are violated (or infringed, or broken, etc.) the aim of language, viz. communication, cannot save *per accidens* be achieved. Rules are laid down in the teaching of language and they are appealed to in the course of criticizing a person's linguistic performance.
>
> The picture admits of variation, of elaboration, but I shall not probe deeper into these mysteries. Such a picture of language can produce, can be the product of, nothing but confusion. An appeal to rules in the course of discussing the regularities to be found in a natural language is as irrelevant as an appeal to the laws of Massachusetts while discussing the laws of motion.[13]

---

[13] *Semantic Analysis* (Ithaca, New York: Cornell University Press, 1960), pp. 34–35.

But if we take the philosophers' rules of language to be tacit conventions of language, we escape Ziff's attack. For we are not supposing that these so-called rules are laid down in the teaching of language—we need not even suppose that language is taught—and we are not supposing that these so-called rules are appealed to in the course of criticizing linguistic performance. Yet our rules will not just be regularities in verbal behavior; they will be regularities in verbal behavior, and in expectations and preferences regarding verbal behavior, and in expectations regarding these expectations and preferences, and so on.

5. Conformative Behavior

David Shwayder, in *The Stratification of Behaviour*,[14] undertakes to give an analysis of a concept of rule. He introduces a correlative concept for the purpose: that of *conformative behavior*. The term is defined explicitly without mentioning rules. Then Shwayder's concept of rule—our ordinary one, he hopes—is defined explicitly in terms of conformative behavior. The two concepts are to be related thus: rules are certain facts that can be reasons for an agent's behavior; "conformative behavior is of a kind which requires that the agent have a certain kind of reason or mistaken reason, which we can schematize as 'That's the rule'" (p. 238). This includes deliberately *not* conforming to a supposed rule; conform*ative* behavior is not limited to conform*ing* behavior.

Shwayder's doctrine of rule and conformative behavior closely resembles my analysis of convention. (Shwayder happens also to use the term "convention," but for something quite different. Since his "convention" is much like H. P. Grice's "meaning$_{nn}$" which I shall discuss in Chapter IV.5, I shall not consider it further.) Behavior that qualifies under my definition as conformity to a convention qualifies under Shwayder's as conformative behavior, and for much the same reasons. But some differences emerge. Conformative behavior in-

[14] New York: Humanities Press, 1965.

cludes conformity to some regularities that are not conventions and that can scarcely even be called rules.

Shwayder leads up to his definition of rules and conformative behavior by stating several theses about rules which ought to follow from any satisfactory theory, and which will follow from his.

(1) Conformative behavior is not merely behavior that happens to conform to rules. "The agent must himself either conform to or act in violation of the rule. A condition for that is his believing that a rule exists" (p. 241).

(2) Some rules must be formulated in advance; others need not be. But in either case the rule itself is distinct from a formulation or statement of that rule.

(3) Rules are not, or not merely, regularities in behavior. Still less are they the generalizations we may frame about regularities in behavior. But regularities in behavior may be due to the existence of rules to which agents regularly conform.

(4) Rules are primarily rules of a community of agents. Conformative behavior presumes community rules. Private rules are possible, but they are somehow secondary to community rules and it is essential that they are capable of becoming community rules.

(5) Rules are certain reasons for acting: they are facts of a certain sort whose supposed existence is a reason for certain behavior, namely, conformative behavior. (This is so even in nonstandard cases in which the agent is mistaken about the existence of a rule or is acting to violate a rule.) A rule is a reason for acting by virtue of some such principle as "one ought to act to conform to rule," "one ought to act to avoid the penalties or discomforts which may ensue upon an infraction or breach of the rule," and so on (p. 251).

Now we reach Shwayder's central thesis about the nature of rules: "Community rules are systems of expectation. An agent conforms to such a rule if he acts for the reason that members of the community are entitled to expect him so to act" (p. 252). He elaborates:

> Confining ourselves to community rule, the idea is this: One
> follows a rule if he conforms to what he sees are the legitimate

expectations of others; and the existence of a rule is, moreover, what entitles the others to their expectations, thus rendering them "legitimate." A community rule exists if the members of a community regulate their affairs according to what other members of the community would legitimately expect them to do. The rule is at once the expectations one conforms to and what legitimizes or warrants those expectations. The rule is, as it were, a system of community, mutual expectation. When one conforms to a rule he acts in the knowledge or belief that others would expect him so to behave. That the others are entitled to those expectations is his reason. Of course one may act in violation of such rules; but even there too one must believe that others have legitimate expectations. If one has no thoughts about what is expected of him, then he can neither conform to nor act in violation of the rule. (p. 253)

But Shwayder has not yet defined conformative behavior to his satisfaction, for he is still mentioning the rule itself. He must find some way to restate his offending condition that "the existence of a rule is . . . what entitles the others to their expectations, thus rendering them 'legitimate.'" It should be the existence of some *feature* of the rule—one that can be otherwise described.

Before Shwayder goes on, though, he temporarily restricts himself to "what is surely the most fundamental and persistently the most common case, that of rules of community, with the additional conditions (1) that some of the members of that community are *present*, where (2) the agents act to *conform*, and (3) the agent and his observers may be taken to *know* all that is relevant to be known about the situation" (p. 254). (The "observers" are extraneous describers of behavior whose concepts Shwayder is examining. So condition [3] is not a common-knowledge condition, and Shwayder is vulnerable to the arguments that led us to establish one.)

Conformative behavior in the fundamental case has so far been described, in effect, as behavior justifiable by the reasoning represented in Figure 31. (Where Shwayder speaks of knowledge, I con-

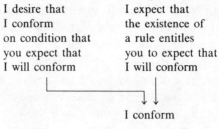

Figure 31

tinue to speak of expectations. But the difference does not matter, since in any normal case the expectations will also be knowledge.) The problem is to redescribe this piece of reasoning in a way that does not mention the rule itself.

Shwayder's solution is given in his formula: "I act from the knowledge that others know that I will act from the knowledge that they expect me so to behave" (p. 256). I take this to mean that there must be part of the agent's justification which is represented by Figure 32. Combining these two fragments of the agent's justification,

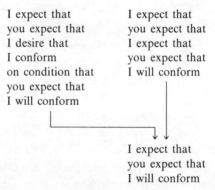

Figure 32

we find that his justification must be represented in part by Figure 33. I take it that an action meets Shwayder's definition of con-formative behavior if and only if it can be justified by reasoning

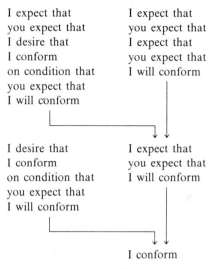

Figure 33

that fits this schema, which we may call the *schema for conformative behavior.*

Shwayder has made the following changes in his condition for conformative behavior. On his first version, I know that the others are entitled to their expectation about my behavior by "the existence of a rule." On his second version, I know that the others are entitled to their expectation about my behavior because they could acquire that expectation by deriving it from their knowledge that I know they expect me so to behave, together with their knowledge that I will try to do what is expected of me. Moreover, it is by replicating just this derivation that *I* could obtain my own knowledge of their expectation about my behavior.

By this change, Shwayder has succeeded in analyzing out his residual mention of the rule. Now that his definition of conformative behavior in the fundamental case is satisfactory, he is free to go on, without circularity, to define *rules* as those mutual expectations about behavior which figure in conformative behavior as reasons for acting.

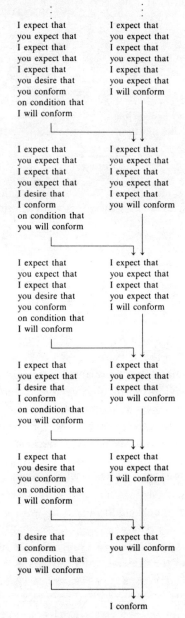

⋮   ⋮

I expect that   I expect that
you expect that   you expect that
I expect that   I expect that
you expect that   you expect that
I expect that   I expect that
you desire that   you will conform
you conform
on condition that
I will conform

I expect that   I expect that
you expect that   you expect that
I expect that   I expect that
you expect that   you expect that
I desire that   I expect that
I conform   you will conform
on condition that
you will conform

I expect that   I expect that
you expect that   you expect that
I expect that   I expect that
you desire that   you expect that
you conform   I will conform
on condition that
I will conform

I expect that   I expect that
you expect that   you expect that
I desire that   I expect that
I conform   you will conform
on condition that
you will conform

I expect that   I expect that
you desire that   you expect that
you conform   I will conform
on condition that
I will conform

I desire that   I expect that
I conform   you will conform
on condition that
you will conform

I conform

Figure 34

They are just those expectations about behavior that the other members of an agent's community have derived in the specified way.

Next Shwayder extends his definitions by relaxing his restrictions on the fundamental case. He defines conformative behavior in which no other members of the agent's community are present; in which the agent is acting to violate a rule; in which the agent is mistaken about the existence of a rule; or in which the rule involved is a private, potentially public rule. But we will not pursue these extensions. For it is Shwayder's doctrine of conformative behavior in the fundamental case that comes closest to my analysis of conformity to convention.

When we take any example of an action conforming to a convention, on my analysis, it will also be found to satisfy Shwayder's definition of conformative behavior in the fundamental case. That is no accident. Whenever I conform to a convention, my action is justifiable by replications; the depth of nesting is limited only by the availability of ancillary premises regarding rationality. Taking the two-person case, for simplicity, and ignoring the use of rationality premises, my justification may be represented by our usual replication schema, as shown in Figure 34. But there is a different way to represent essentially the same justification of my action. Consider any two consecutive stages of the above schema. Together they take me from an $(n + 2)$th-order expectation about action to an nth-order expectation about action (or, if $n = 0$, a decision to act) via an intermediate $(n + 1)$th-order expectation about action. But the same reasoning—same premises, same conclusion—could be carried out in a different order, with a different intermediate step. The last two stages, for instance, could be rearranged as shown in Figure 35. The same premises lead me to the same action, but the premises are used in a different order. There is a new intermediate step—I derive the desire to conform on condition that you expect me to. Given that, my expectation that you will conform becomes superflous. Rearranging each pair of stages from the bottom up, we obtain the *rearranged replication schema* shown in Figure 36. And now we can

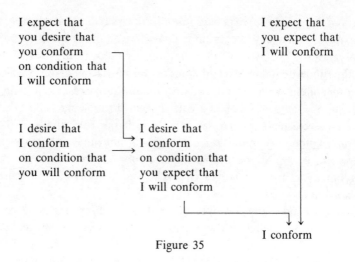

I expect that
you desire that
you conform
on condition that
I will conform

I expect that
you expect that
I will conform

I desire that
I conform
on condition that
you will conform

I desire that
I conform
on condition that
you expect that
I will conform

I conform

Figure 35

see that the schema for conformative behavior is just the central part (within the boundary) of the rearranged replication schema. It follows that any action in conformity to a convention, being justifiable by replications and hence by rearranged replications, meets Shwayder's definition of conformative behavior.

The converse does not hold, however. Suppose I want to conform if others expect me to, but without regard to anything *they* will do *because* they expect me to conform. Then the justification of my action cannot fit the rearranged replication schema. Since the left-hand column will be missing, my action cannot be conformity to a convention. But my justification might still fit the schema for conformative behavior. If so, my action would be conformative behavior. I would be the only *agent* in the situation; the others would be involved merely as supposed holders of expectations about me. I might just be trying to prove to myself that I can live up to others' expectations if I want to. I might want to get them to think me a dull, predictable fellow. I might want to avoid disappointing or surprising them. In any of these cases, I may behave as I do "from the knowledge that others know that I will act from the knowledge

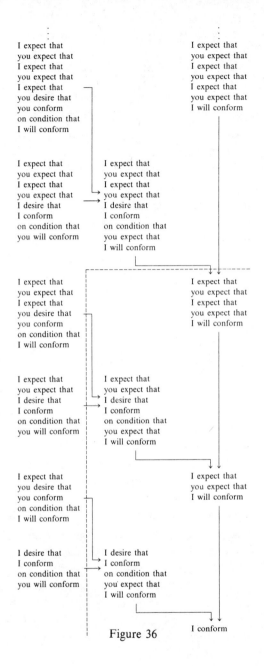

Figure 36

115

that they expect me so to behave." But these cases of conformative behavior seem to be cases Shwayder did not intend. They do not fit his formula, "I act for the reason 'That's the rule.'" I *do* act for the reason "That's their legitimate exception"—and the legitimacy is of the right sort—but their legitimate expectation in such a case cannot possibly be called a rule.

Shwayder has gained some generality by requiring only a central fragment, not the whole, of the rearranged replication schema. But it is not clear why this generality is desirable. And to buy it, he has left out an important fact about the intended sort of conformative behavior: namely, that I want to conform to your expectations *because of* the way I expect you to act on your expectations. If I thought you would not act on your expectations, I would concern myself with how you would act, not with what you expect. When this fact is left out of the story, our understanding of the phenomenon is badly distorted.

There is a second way for an action to be conformative behavior without being conformity to convention, even if the justification of the action does fit the whole rearranged replication schema. Justification by replications, and hence justification by rearranged replications, applies to *any* action that is part of a proper equilibrium. But the equilibrium does not have to be in a coordination problem, and it does not have to be a coordination equilibrium. It might even be a unique equilibrium in a game of pure conflict.

Suppose that for some reason pairs of us must often play the game of penny matching with an option of "calling off," a game represented by the payoff matrix shown in Figure 37. This is a game of pure conflict: Row-chooser and Column-chooser must play simultaneously by calling off the game (*R1* or *C1*), by putting down a penny head up (*R2* or *C2*), or by putting down a penny tail up (*R3* or *C3*). If the pennies match, Column-chooser takes them both. If they fail to match, Row-chooser takes them both. If both players call off, each keeps his penny. If only one calls off, the other pays him a halfpenny. There is a unique equilibrium ⟨*R1*, *C1*⟩; it is not a coordination equilibrium.

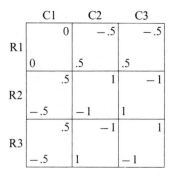

Figure 37

I should call off unless I am quite confident that you will play heads (or tails), in which case I should play heads or tails (as appropriate) to beat you. In particular, I prefer to call off if you will. If we play often, then once the nature of the game has become common knowledge between us, we call off every time. It is common knowledge between us that we call off, and that we do so because we expect each other to.

When I call off, my action is conformative behavior. Its justification fits the rearranged replication schema and *a fortiori* the schema for conformative behavior. I am acting from the knowledge that you are entitled to expect me to call off, or—more precisely—that you know I will act from the knowledge that you expect me to call off.

But our regularity of calling off does not meet the definition of convention. Its exclusion is justified by two important differences between it and clear cases of convention: (1) The players' equilibria are not coordination equilibria. They are not cooperation in the common interest, but deadlocked compromises between completely opposed interests. Neither is satisfied with $\langle R1, C1 \rangle$. Neither could have achieved a better outcome by acting otherwise himself, but each wishes the other had acted otherwise. (2) The players' equilibria are the only possible ones. There is nothing arbitrary about them. There is no other possible way to play with sound strategy and accurate mutual expectations. Nor would it be natural to call our regularity a rule, except insofar as *any* regularity or any strategic maxim may sometimes be called a rule (and Shwayder certainly does not want to be that inclusive). This must be another kind of conformative behavior that Shwayder did not intend, for it is not—intuitively—action for the reason "That's the rule."

A last difference between Shwayder's rules and my conventions deserves to be mentioned only because the reader may have noticed it already. For Shwayder, a rule is a system of expectations likely to produce regular behavior. For me, a convention is a regularity in behavior produced by a system of expectations. Shwayder wants to allow (in one of his extensions from the fundamental case) for rules that are mostly broken; this generality may be plausible for his analysandum "rule," but not for my analysandum "convention." I am concerned with cases in which we have both the regularity and the expectations, and in such cases the regularity is the central thing. But the difference is superficial. It would vanish if we recast our analyses in the form, "A rule (convention) exists if and only if . . . "—not "A rule (convention) is . . ."

6. Imitation

Someone who is party to a convention conforms to a regularity because he has an interest in conforming if certain others do and because he believes—rightly—that they do. He acts as he does because he expects the others so to act. In short, he imitates them. But we should not conclude that any regularity which originates or persists by some sort of mutual imitation is therefore a convention. There are several cases in which each member of some population acts in conformity to some regularity because the others do and that regularity is nevertheless not a convention.

Sometimes people copy each other's actions—say, mannerisms—more or less unaware that they are doing so. Given a group composed entirely of such people, a mannerism can spread and persist by mutual imitation. But there is no preference involved on anyone's part (unless we count every inclination as a transient preference). Each simply does something, not caring and scarcely knowing whether he does it or not. So *a fortiori* his action does not answer to any interest in so acting if the others do. The regularity produced is not a convention.

Sometimes people copy each other's preferences. A coffee drinker put among tea drinkers may somehow come to prefer tea. It is not that he prefers to drink coffee if the others drink coffee and tea if the others drink tea. At first he preferred coffee regardless of what the others preferred; later he prefers tea just as unconditionally. But it was his exposure to the tea drinkers that caused him to change. We can tell we are dealing with changeable unconditional preferences, not fixed conditional preferences, by observing a lag in his adaptation; or by observing his preferences regarding such things as a gamble that will entitle him to an unlimited supply of tea if all his neighbors switch to coffee. Given a group composed entirely of preference copiers, preferences and the actions answering to them could spread and persist by mutual imitation. But the regularity so produced would not be a convention, since the actions conforming to it would answer to an unconditional preference.

Sometimes people trust each other's practical judgments: crediting others with probably having good reasons for what they are doing, I may infer from their actions that they know something I do not—something that is a good reason for me to do the same. I may wear my raincoat because others do, thinking that probably they are wearing raincoats because they have heard a forecast of rain. This sort of imitation involves neither change of preferences nor preferences that are conditional on others' actions. Before and after I saw my neighbors in raincoats, my preference was to wear my raincoat if and only if it was going to rain. And that is my preference without regard to what others do. Their wearing of raincoats makes me wear one because I take their actions as evidence: evidence of their expectation of rain and therefore (indirectly, through my standing beliefs about the likely causes of their expectations) evidence that it is likely to rain. A regularity might spread and persist in a group of people by just this sort of mutual imitation. It might happen one day that *everyone* in town wears his raincoat because he sees the others wearing theirs and infers—reasonably enough, perhaps,[15] but falsely—that they probably heard a forecast of rain. (The one who started it all must be an exception at first, since he put on his raincoat while the others were not wearing theirs. But whatever his original reason was, if he keeps his raincoat on later because he sees the others wearing theirs, he becomes just like the rest.) This regularity is not a convention; the preference that sustains it is not conditional on others' conforming.

Even when people do imitate each other because of their conditional preference for doing something if the others do, still the regularity that persists by this mutual imitation is not necessarily a convention. For the situation may not be one in which coincidence of interests predominates over conflict. Some sort of equilibrium is sustained, but it may not be a *coordination* equilibrium. In the example of pure conflict from the preceding section, for instance, each has a conditional preference for calling off if the other does. This preference permits a regularity whereby each calls off every time because the other does so. But we saw that this regularity is not a convention; although each is satisfied with his own choice (given his opponent's), neither is satisfied with his opponent's choice (given his own). Each wants to conform to the regularity of always calling off if the other also conforms to it; but each would like better to conform while the other does not. In the case of a genuine convention, on the other hand, each wants to conform if the others do, and each wants the others to conform if he does.

Now we have distinguished five pure species of regularity sustained by mutual imitation: convention itself and four counterfeits. They

[15] It may be that everyone was completely reasonable in inferring and acting as he did—although no one will think so when he learns what happened. The manifest irrationality of the group may not be due to any irrationality of its members. It is no mistake to expect rain when one sees people in raincoats, despite the bad results of doing so this time.

differ in the kind of imitation involved, the process whereby actions produce similar actions by others. Each case considered so far involves a single kind of imitation; but there could equally well be hybrids, regularities sustained by mutual imitation of several kinds mixed in varying proportions. It seems plausible that fashions, fads, panics, riots, and bandwagons as we know them are produced by several sorts of mutual imitation working together. Suppose we are wearing beige ties this year, each because the others do. Morgan follows the fashion without knowing he is doing so; when he picks a tie haphazardly, he just happens to pick the beige one. Jones is wearing beige ties because he likes the color; but, unknown to him, his tastes are caused by the prevailing fashion and will change with it. Griffith wears a beige tie because he falsely supposes the other beige wearers to have discovered some special functional virtue in beige which will benefit him too. Owen and Thomas both want to wear whatever color of tie the others will wear; but Owen hopes to find occasional nonconformists he can laugh at, whereas Thomas hopes there will be no nonconformists. Every man after his fashion follows the fashion, and the wearing of beige ties persists and spreads by mutual imitation of mixed kinds.

I do not count it a regularity by mutual imitation when a good idea catches on. Such a regularity spreads by imitation, as people see what others are doing and realize they would benefit by doing the same. But the imitation is not mutual—no two people learned the trick from each other—and the regularity does not persist by imitation. Once he starts, each goes on because he benefits by what he is doing whether other people go on doing it or not.

IV | Convention and Communication

1. Sample Signals

So far we have been considering conventions in general. Now we turn to one especially important class of conventions: those whereby we give to suitable actions the status of signals.

Communication by conventional signals is a commonplace phenomenon, so much so that we must make an effort not to take it for granted. We could exercise our tacit understanding all we want without ever making it more explicit. That is what would happen if we started by saying that actions are signals when we endow them with meanings. This truism will bring us no nearer to describing the phenomenon of signaling without depending on our prior tacit understanding thereof. So let us describe the phenomenon in other terms and leave meaning to look after itself.

Consider a communicator and his audience—for instance, the sexton of the Old North Church and Paul Revere. The sexton acts according to some contingency plan, such as:

> $R1$: If the redcoats are observed staying home, hang no lantern in the belfry.
>
> If the redcoats are observed setting out by land, hang one lantern in the belfry.
>
> If the redcoats are observed setting out by sea, hang two lanterns in the belfry.

or

> $R2$: If the redcoats are observed staying home, hang one lantern in the belfry.

> If the redcoats are observed setting out by land, hang two lanterns in the belfry.
>
> If the redcoats are observed setting out by sea, hang no lantern in the belfry.

or

> *R3*: If the redcoats are observed staying home, hang one lantern in the belfry.
>
> If the redcoats are observed setting out by land, hang no lantern in the belfry.
>
> If the redcoats are observed setting out by sea, hang two lanterns in the belfry.

(There are three more contingency plans with no lantern, one lantern, and two lanterns, plus any number of further plans involving other actions—hanging three lanterns, hanging colored lanterns, waving lanterns, hanging a flag, etc.) Paul Revere acts according to a contingency plan, such as:

> *C1*: If no lantern is observed hanging in the belfry, go home.
>
> If one lantern is observed hanging in the belfry, warn the countryside that the redcoats are coming by land.
>
> If two lanterns are observed hanging in the belfry, warn the countryside that the redcoats are coming by sea.

or

> *C2*: If no lantern is observed hanging in the belfry, warn the countryside that the redcoats are coming by sea.
>
> If one lantern is observed hanging in the belfry, go home.
>
> If two lanterns are observed hanging in the belfry, warn the countryside that the redcoats are coming by land.

or

> *C3*: If no lantern is observed hanging in the belfry, warn the countryside that the redcoats are coming by land.
>
> If one lantern is observed hanging in the belfry, go home.
>
> If two lanterns are observed hanging in the belfry, warn the countryside that the redcoats are coming by sea.

It matters little to either which contingency plan he follows, provided their two plans combine to ensure that Paul Revere warns the countryside that the redcoats are coming by land if and only if the sexton observes them setting out by land, and that Paul Revere warns the countryside that the redcoats are coming by sea if and only if the sexton observes them setting out by sea (so far as interference and error permit). Each must act according to a contingency plan chosen with regard to his expectation about the other's choice—an expectation formed, in this case, by an explicit agreement. Their situation is a coordination problem represented in Figure 38. Successful com-

	C1	C2	C3 ...
R1	1 1	0 0	.5 .5
R2	0 0	1 1	.5 .5
R3 ⋮	.5 .5	.5 .5	1 1

Figure 38

munication occurs if they achieve one of the coordination equilibria; for instance, the historical $\langle R1, C1 \rangle$, or $\langle R2, C2 \rangle$, $\langle R3, C3 \rangle$ ... These combinations ensure that Paul Revere will give the right warning. Conditionally successful communication occurs if they achieve one of the combinations like $\langle R1, C3 \rangle$: Paul Revere may or may not give the right warning, depending on what the redcoats do. The outright failures are combinations like $\langle R1, C2 \rangle$, which ensure that Paul Revere will give a wrong warning no matter what.

I have now described the character of a case of signaling without mentioning the meaning of the signals: that two lanterns meant that the redcoats were coming by sea, or whatever. But nothing important seems to have been left unsaid, so what has been said must somehow imply that the signals have their meanings.

It should not disturb us that this is a problem of coordinating contingency plans, not—as in the previous coordination problems—of coordinating actions themselves. We are treating the agent's *choice* of a contingency plan as an action—one that is part of his action of choosing a contingency plan and then acting on it. An agent's action according to a contingency plan is regarded as consisting of two phases: choice of a contingency plan and fulfillment of the chosen plan. His choice is concentrated in the first phase; his use of his ability to tell which contingency holds is concentrated in the second. The agents' coordination problem pertains only to the first phase. For instance, if the sexton hangs two lanterns after observing the redcoats setting out by sea, he might be doing it according to *R1* or *R3* or any number of other contingency plans. We count the difference in contingency plan as making a difference in his action, even though it is a difference that turns out not to matter.

In this case, the sexton and Paul Revere agreed upon signals for a single occasion. In other cases, the same signaling system—preeminently analogous coordination equilibrium combinations of contingency plans for a communicator and an audience—may occur repeatedly, without need for fresh agreement every time. The regularity whereby communicators and audiences use such a pair of contingency plans is a convention.

Let us consider five examples of signaling conventions.

(1) The International Code of Signals lists a correspondence of flag hoists and certain predicaments. That is, it gives a contingency plan for ships (strictly, for ships' officers) of the form: if in such-and-such predicament, hoist such-and-such flags. There is a complementary contingency plan for ships that observe flags on nearby ships: if a ship hoists such-and-such flags, act as would be appropriate on the assumption that it is in such-and-such predicament. Ships do regularly act according to these two complementary plans. A ship on a speed

trial hoists a flag white on the left and blue on the right, and other ships seeing that flag keep out of her way. A ship loading or unloading explosives hoists a flag white on the left and red on the right, and other ships seeing that flag take appropriate precautions. A ship whose crew has mutinied hoists a flag with a yellow cross on red above a flag with diagonal yellow and red stripes, and other ships seeing those flags give whatever help they can.

The regularity of acting according to this pair of contingency plans is a convention. Any ship does conform when she is in one of the designated predicaments or when she observes flags on nearby ships. And she conforms because she expects other ships to conform too— specifically, those other ships related to her as communicator to audience or as audience to communicator—and she prefers to conform to this, or any similar, regularity if they do. They share this preference. And it is common knowledge among ships that these conditions hold.

The convention governing flag hoists is a relatively formal affair. It originated by explicit agreement among representatives of some of those now party to it; it is explicitly codified; violations are punishable independently of conformity by others. For instance, a ship might be held responsible for an accident if she had failed to hoist the prescribed flag, even if that part of the code had fallen into disuse. But if it is important that ships respond appropriately to others' predicaments, then once again this independent incentive would be redundant if it agreed with convention, would be outweighed if it did not, would not be decisive either way, and therefore would not detract from the conventionality of the code.

(2) Now we turn to a very informal signaling convention: that whereby a helper standing behind a truck gestures to the driver to help him steer the truck into a narrow space. Here there is no agreement, no authoritative reference book, no institutionalized enforcement, no teaching. But the elements of a system of conventional signals are here: the helper's gestures depend on the position of the truck and the driver's steering depends on the helper's observed

gestures. So the steering depends mediately on the position of the truck, and this dependence is such as to serve the common interest of the helper and the driver in getting the truck into the space.

The helper could have made his gestures depend differently on the position of the truck. The driver could have made his steering depend differently on the helper's gestures. Some of the other combinations of dependences would have given the same dependence of the steering on the position of the truck, and would have done about as well for getting the truck into the space. The helper gestures as he does because he expects the driver to respond as he does, and the driver responds as he does because he expects the helper to gesture as he does. They have derived these expectations from their experience with helpers and drivers in the past who set a precedent by gesturing and responding according to the same dependences.

Their behavior conforms to a conventional regularity. It would be a hard regularity to describe, if only because it is hard to describe a gesture or a way of steering well enough to identify it. Yet experienced helpers and drivers do conform, expect conformity, and recognize conformity, presumably without the aid of descriptions of their regular behavior.

We can say that helpers and drivers among us act according to their respective contingency plans, provided we understand that these contingency plans are no more than descriptions that *could be given* of the way their actions depend upon their observations. In example (1) the communicator's and audience's contingency plans were more than this: they were descriptions that *had been given* of a dependence between predicaments and flags, and the dependence was maintained partly because the agents could consult that description to find out what to do.

There must, in general, be some mediating mechanism to make an agent's actions depend on his observations in a definite way. The mechanism must be sufficiently under the agent's control that he can set it to produce the dependence he wants. *One* such mechanism is a description of the desired dependence for the agent to consult. But in the present example, we have no reason to think that the helper's or the driver's dependence-producing mechanism contains a description of his desired dependence, or anything like one.

Our first two examples illustrated the standard sort of signaling, in formal and informal versions. The third is a slight variation; the fourth, fifth, and sixth are more serious ones.

(3) A man blazes a trail by making marks that depend on the route he thinks it best for others to take. His actions are done once and for all, but their traces last a long time. When others follow his trail afterwards, the route they take depends on the observed traces of his actions, so that they take the route he thought best for them.

In the previous examples we had sequences of independent coordination problems between communicator-audience pairs. In this example, each trail gives us many two-person coordination problems with the trail blazer's side in common. The several trail followers must all choose their contingency plans to achieve coordination with the trail blazer's original choice of a contingency plan. The trail blazer must choose his contingency plan to achieve coordination with each—or as many as possible—of the trail followers' choices of contingency plans on various occasions. There are as many different coordination problems as there are occasions on which the trail is followed. These coordination problems are extended through time, so that the trail followers must have contingency plans for responding to the observed traces of the trail blazer's actions, not to observations of those actions themselves.

(4) A railroad installs automatic signals: semaphores and the machinery to make their position depend on the occupancy of the track ahead. Instead of a communicator who does observable actions according to a contingency plan, there is the original agent who acts to install the machinery and there is the machinery which subsequently operates according to a contingency plan. As in example (3), there are any number of two-person coordination problems with one side—that of the agent who chose a contingency plan to be built into the machinery—in common. But in this example the agent who

chooses a contingency plan for the signaling machinery does not himself act according to that plan.

Or the trains which stop and go on in response to the semaphores could be automated. On a railroad with automated trains and manual semaphores, every agent who operates a semaphore is involved in a two-person coordination problem with the agent who chose, once and for all, a contingency plan to be built into the trains. (On a railroad with both automated trains and automated semaphores, there is only the single coordination problem between the agent who chooses a contingency plan to be built into the trains and the agent who chooses a contingency plan to be built into the semaphores.)

(5) An automatic stoplight is installed to regulate traffic at a crossroad. The light always shows red to one road, green to the other. It changes periodically, not according to any contingency plan. The drivers at the crossroad (at any time) *do* act according to a conventional contingency plan: stop on red, go on green. Thereby they get through the crossing safely and easily. The drivers—the stoplight's audience—achieve a coordination equilibrium. (Once more the independent incentives provided by the highway patrol are superflous if they agree with convention, outweighed if not, and hence do not make the regularity any less conventional.)

In this case the coordination is entirely among members of the audience. No one plays the role of communicator, neither the stoplight nor whoever had it installed. Nobody chose a contingency plan for the stoplight; it has none. It is just a feature of the scene which the drivers can use to mediate their own coordination. It is inessential that someone is responsible for its presence: if we built everlasting stoplights and our descendants forgot they were artifacts, the lights could still regulate traffic and they would still be signals. Even the rising of the moon can be a signal—to begin an uprising, say—though it would be a prearranged one-shot signal, not a conventional one.

(6) Many men take turns using the same horses. When they want to turn a team right they yell "gee"; when they want to turn a team left they yell "haw." When a horse fails to turn right on "gee" or

left on "haw," they hit him. The men are the communicators and the horses are the audience, and both act according to complementary contingency plans. But the coordination problem of choosing contingency plans, and the convention that solves it, exist only among the men. The horses are only beasts, and they react as they have been trained to react. The men must coordinate in order to keep the horses trained and in order to take advantage of their training.

2. Analysis of Signaling

Now that we have made the acquaintance of signaling problems, signaling systems, and signaling conventions, how shall we define them?

In this section I shall limit my discussion to *two-sided* signaling, in which the coordination needed is coordination between communicator and audience. The example of Paul Revere and the sexton, and the first three examples of signaling conventions, were two-sided. The last three examples illustrated *one-sided* signaling, in which the coordination needed was either between communicators or between members of the audience. Having defined two-sided signaling problems, systems, and conventions, it would be straightforward but tedious to give the analogous definitions for both kinds of one-sided signaling and for signaling in which a mixture of two-sided and one-sided coordination is needed. I shall leave it to the examples to show how that would be done. But what is said about signaling henceforth is meant to apply *mutatis mutandis* to signaling in general.

A *two-sided signaling problem* is a situation S involving an agent called the *communicator* and one or more other agents called the *audience*, such that it is true that, and it is common knowledge for the communicator and the audience that:

> Exactly one of several alternative states of affairs $s_1 \ldots s_m$ holds. The communicator, but not the audience, is in a good position to tell which one it is.

Each member of the audience can do any one of several alternative actions $r_1 \ldots r_m$ called *responses*. Everyone involved wants the audience's responses to depend in a certain way upon the state of affairs that holds. There is a certain one-to-one function F from $\{s_i\}$ onto $\{r_j\}$ such that everyone prefers that each member of the audience do $F(s_i)$ on condition that s_i holds, for each s_i.

The communicator can do any one of several alternative actions $\sigma_1 \ldots \sigma_n$ ($n \geq m$) called *signals*. The audience is in a good position to tell which one he does. No one involved has any preference regarding these actions which is strong enough to outweigh his preference for the dependence F of audience's responses upon states of affairs.

Note that the preferred response is specified to be the same for all members of the audience. This may seem restrictive, but it is not. If the preferred action of a member of the audience depends on his circumstances, his role in the situation, or anything else besides the state of affairs in $\{s_i\}$, that dependence should be built into the specifications of the responses $\{r_j\}$. If a warship is in distress, another warship's preferred response may be this: to take her place in battle if it is possible to do so effectively; otherwise to come to her aid. We count this as one response, specified by a pair of conditionals.

A *communicator's contingency plan* is any possible way in which the communicator's signal may depend upon the state of affairs that he observes to hold. It is a function Fc from $\{s_i\}$ into $\{\sigma_k\}$. A communicator in S acts according to Fc if, for each s_i, he does $Fc(s_i)$ if he observes that s_i holds. Since he is in a position to tell which s_i does hold, and since $Fc(s_i)$ is his own action, he should be able to act according to any contingency plan Fc. If Fc is a one-to-one function, we call it *admissible*.

Similarly, an *audience's contingency plan* is any possible way in which the response of a member of the audience may depend upon the signal he observes the communicator to give. It is a one-to-one function Fa from part of $\{\sigma_k\}$ into $\{r_j\}$. A member of the audience in S acts according to Fa if, for each σ_k in the domain of Fa, he does $Fa(\sigma_k)$ if he observes that the communicator gives σ_k. Since he is in a position to tell which σ_k is given, and since $Fa(\sigma_k)$ is his own action, he should be able to act according to any contingency plan Fa. If the range of Fa coincides with the range of F, we call Fa *admissible*.

Suppose the communicator acts according to a contingency plan Fc and all members of the audience act according to a contingency plan Fa. Then the audience's response will depend on the state of affairs that holds according to the function $Fa|Fc$ obtained by composition of Fa and Fc. (For any two functions f and g, and any argument x such that $g(x)$ is in the domain of f, $f|g(x)$ is defined as $f(g(x))$; $f|g$ is undefined on other arguments.)

If the actual state of affairs happens to be s, and if $Fa|Fc(s) = F(s)$, the audience's response will be one that is preferred in the actual state of affairs. So each agent will be acting according to one of the contingency plans which is best given the others' contingency plans and the actual state of affairs.

Better, suppose $Fa|Fc = F$ uniformly over $\{s_i\}$. (It follows that the range of Fc must coincide with the domain of Fa.) Then the audience's response will be one that is preferred in the actual state of affairs, no matter which state of affairs in $\{s_i\}$ that may happen to be. Each agent will be acting according to the contingency plan that is best given the others' contingency plans and *any* state of affairs. Whenever Fc and Fa combine in this way to give the preferred dependence of the audience's response upon the state of affairs, we call $\langle Fc, Fa \rangle$ a *signaling system*.

All and only admissible contingency plans belong to signaling systems. Proof:

Let Fc be a communicator's contingency plan. If it is admissible, it is one-to-one and it has an inverse $F\check{c}$; if so, $\langle Fc, F|F\check{c} \rangle$ is a signaling system. If it is inadmissible it is not one-to-one; so for any Fa, either $Fa|Fc$ is not one-to-one or $Fa|Fc$ is not defined for some state of affairs; in neither case can $Fa \mid Fc$ coincide with F; so $\langle Fc, Fa \rangle$ is not a signaling system.

Let Fa be an audience's contingency plan. If it is admissible, let $F\breve{a}$ be its inverse; $\langle F\breve{a} \mid F, Fa \rangle$ is a signaling system. If it is inadmissible its range does not coincide with the range of F; so for any Fc, the range of $Fa \mid Fc$ does not coincide with the range of F; so $\langle Fc, Fa \rangle$ is not a signaling system.

In a signaling problem with m states of affairs and n signals, there are $n!/(n - m)!$ signaling systems. Proof:

Construct Fc thus: for any s in $\{s_i\}$, if $F(s)$ is the kth member of the range of F, let $Fc(s)$ be σ_k. Fc is an admissible communicator's contingency plan.

Take any function G which maps the range of Fc one-to-one into $\{\sigma_k\}$. Let $\breve{G}$ be the inverse of G; let $F\breve{c}$ be the inverse of Fc. Then $\langle G \mid Fc, (F \mid F\breve{c}) \mid \breve{G} \rangle$ is a signaling system. Every signaling system can be obtained in this way. There are $n!/(n - m)!$ different one-to-one functions from the range of Fc into $\{\sigma_k\}$, so there are that many different signaling systems.

We may think of the communicator and the audience as acting by first choosing contingency plans and then acting according to their chosen plans. If so, their choices of plans make a coordination problem. We can represent it by a matrix in which the rows represent the communicator's contingency plans and the columns, levels, and so on, represent contingency plans for all members of the audience. Some of these plans are admissible, others are not. An agent's payoff for any combination depends on his payoffs for that combination in each of the states of affairs in $\{s_i\}$, weighted by the probabilities he assigns to the different states of affairs. (For some combinations, we will have to consider what he expects members of the audience to do in response to a signal not in the domains of their chosen plans.) It is easy to see that every signaling system is a proper coordination equilibrium in this coordination problem.

But signaling systems may not be the only coordination equilibria. Certain pairs of inadmissible contingency plans may be coordination equilibria. In our example of Paul Revere and the sexton, suppose a defense against a land attack would also work fairly well against a sea attack, but not vice versa, and suppose the two attacks seem equally likely. Then there may be a coordination equilibrium between this plan for the sexton:

> If the redcoats are observed staying home, hang no lantern in the belfry.
> If the redcoats are observed setting out by land, hang one lantern in the belfry.
> If the redcoats are observed setting out by sea, hang one lantern in the belfry.

and this plan for Paul Revere:

> If no lantern is observed hanging in the belfry, go home.
> If one lantern is observed hanging in the belfry, warn the countryside that the redcoats are coming by land.

The plans combine to give a dependence of Paul Revere's response upon the observed state of affairs which, although not the preferred dependence, is not too bad. But neither one can reach the preferred dependence just by changing his plan; each is acting according to a plan that is best given the other's plan. So the combination is a coordination equilibrium. (It is improper; given the sexton's plan, Paul Revere might just as well have chosen a different plan:

> If no lantern is observed hanging in the belfry, go home.
> If one lantern is observed hanging in the belfry, warn the countryside that the redcoats are coming by land.
> If two lanterns are observed hanging in the belfry, warn the countryside that the redcoats are coming by sea.

His response would have been just the same, no matter what the sexton observed.) It is not a signaling system. At least, it is not a signaling system in our *original* signaling problem. If we reclassify states of affairs and responses, forgetting the difference between the two kinds of attacks and the two kinds of warnings, we get a new signaling problem with a less detailed preferred dependence function; and in this new problem, the combination of plans we are considering is a signaling system and is a proper coordination equilibrium.

So we have two kinds of coordination equilibria in signaling problems. There are signaling systems; and there are improper coordination equilibria that are not signaling systems but would become signaling systems under a less detailed classification of states of affairs and responses. I do not know whether there can be coordination equilibria of any other kind. One relevant result is this: if the audience has just one member, then no combination of one admissible plan and one inadmissible plan can be an equilibrium; for another combination on the same row or column would be a signaling system and would be preferred to the given combination.

Given the definition of signaling systems, we can define a *signaling convention* as any convention whereby members of a population P who are involved as communicators or audience in a certain signaling problem S do their parts of a certain signaling system $\langle Fc, Fa \rangle$ by acting according to their respective contingency plans. If such a convention exists, we also call $\langle Fc, Fa \rangle$ a *conventional signaling system*.

If some signaling problems do turn out to have coordination equilibria that are not signaling systems—not even under a suitable less detailed classification of states of affairs and responses—then we would have to say that there could be conventions which are not signaling conventions even though they govern the choice of contingency plans in a signaling problem. I see no great harm, however, in leaving that possibility open.

When an agent acts in conformity to a signaling convention—and in any other case in which he solves a signaling problem by agreement, salience, or precedent—his action is justified by the reasoning shown in Figure 39 (for a communicator) or in Figure 40 (for a

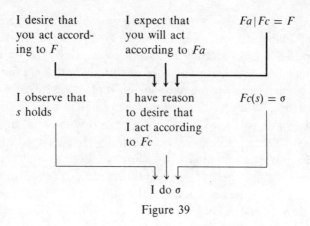

Figure 39

member of the audience). That is, we are treating the agent's choice of an action as a rational choice of a whole contingency plan, followed by action to carry out his chosen plan in the light of particular information about the situation. This is the best treatment when we want to include signaling within the general theory of coordination and convention.

But we could treat the agents' justifications of their choices more economically. The particular information the agent needs—which

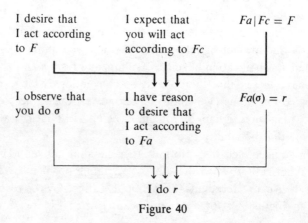

Figure 40

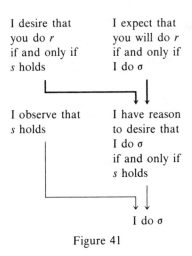

Figure 41

state of affairs holds or which signal was given—is available to him all along; so his choice is justified if he justifies only the relevant part of his contingency plan. Throwing out the irrelevant contingencies, we get the reasoning shown in Figure 41 (for a communicator) or in Figure 42 (for a member of the audience). These justifi-

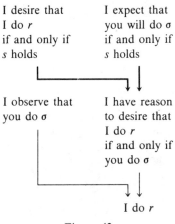

Figure 42

cations may be rearranged slightly, to eliminate the choice of even part of a contingency plan. The premises available can be applied in a different order. For the communicator, we then get the reasoning shown in Figure 43. For a member of the audience, we get the

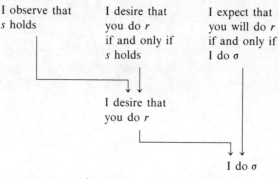

Figure 43

reasoning shown in Figure 44. In the communicator's case, the state of affairs *s* gives him a reason for trying to produce the audience's response *r*; and his expectation that the audience will respond to σ according to *Fa* gives him reason to believe that σ would be an

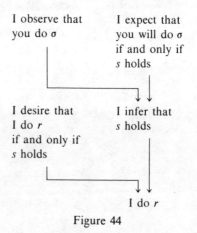

Figure 44

effective means of producing r. So he does σ. In the case of a member of the audience, his expectation that the communicator will act according to Fc gives him reason to take σ as good evidence that s holds; and having inferred that s holds, he has reason to do r.

These new schemata of justification, like the old ones, can be replicated; one agent's replication of the other's reasoning provides him with the central premise for his own reasoning. But these replications must be conditional: one agent figures out how the other *would* reason if he were given a premise. The communicator figures out how the audience would reason in response to a signal; the audience figures out how the communicator would reason in response to a state of affairs. These conditional replications can be replicated in turn—and so on, for any number of stages. Consider the communicator's reasoning in justification of his decision to give σ; we can carry it two stages back, as shown in Figure 45.

We have now represented the agents' justifications in two quite different ways. The first way is based on the fact that the agent's choices of contingency plan constitute a coordination problem, and the conventional signaling system $\langle Fc, Fa \rangle$ is a coordination equilibrium therein. The second way is based on the fact that, since it is common knowledge that the audience acts according to Fa, it is common knowledge that a signal σ is a good means of producing the response $Fa(\sigma)$; and that, since it is common knowledge that the communicator acts according to Fc, it is common knowledge that a signal σ is good evidence that the state holds which is mapped onto σ by Fc.

Both representations are somewhat artificial, however, as representations of an agent's *actual* reasoning. Fortunately, they are artificial in opposite and complementary ways. So if one is realistic, the other is not. Take an agent who does not merely follow his chosen contingency plan blindly. After he knows which is the actual contingency, he deliberates on the likely outcomes of his alternative actions and does the one that seems best. Must he really be said to choose—or renew his choice of—his whole contingency plan? Or only the part

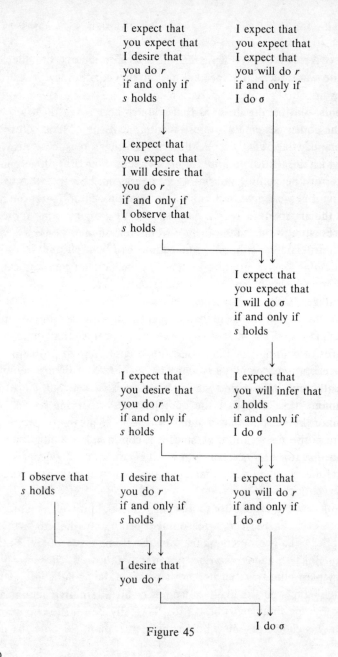

Figure 45

that covers the actual contingency? Take, on the other hand, an agent whose signaling is dull routine work, done with his mind elsewhere. Does he stop to think: "This action will get the audience to do so-and-so, which is the best thing under the circumstances, so I had better do this action" (if he is a communicator), or "The communicator must be doing that because he has observed such-and-such, in which case this would be the best action for me to do, so I had better do this action" (if he is in the audience)? No: he relaxes and follows his contingency plan by habit. He is aware in a general way that the plan he is following is the best one, given the plan his partner is following. If he received evidence to the contrary, he would stop and think, and he would begin to act according to a different contingency plan. But as long as matters go well, he does not think about how what he is doing will be for the best on any particular occasion.

But we do not have to represent the agents' actual reasoning. We have to consider only the rational justifications of their choices by practical reasoning they *could* go through, given their beliefs and desires. Yet this is not to renounce an interest in explaining their choices. Justifications do explain choices, whether or not the agent actually goes through a process of reasoning following the justification. For it is a fact of human nature that we tend to act in ways justified by our beliefs and desires, even when we do not think through the justification. I may put it negatively: whatever may be the habitual processes that actually do control our choices, if they started tending to go against our beliefs and desires they soon would be overridden, corrected, and retrained by explicit practical reasoning.

3. Verbal Signaling

An action is suited to be a signal if it or its traces are easy for an audience to observe; and if it is intrinsically unimportant, so that no party has strong extraneous preferences for or against its being done.

Two sorts of actions are ideally suited to be signals, in many situations: production of a string of vocal sounds within earshot of the audience; and production of a string of lasting marks on a smooth surface that will be visible to the audience. In short, speaking and writing.

Let us define a *verbal expression* as any finite sequence of types of vocal sounds or types of marks.[1] To utter or to inscribe a verbal expression is to produce a string of sounds reverberating in the air or a string of marks on a surface. A signal that is an action of uttering or inscribing a verbal expression may be called a *verbal signal*.

Officially, the signal is the action. But we usually need not be careful to distinguish the action, the string of sounds or marks produced by the action, and the verbal expression uttered or inscribed; all three can be called the signal. We can also allow "uttering" to cover inscribing as well as vocal uttering.

Had circumstances been otherwise, the sexton and Paul Revere might have found it best to use a prearranged or conventional verbal signaling system. As a signal to be given if the redcoats were observed setting out by sea, the sexton might have whispered sounds in Paul Revere's ear or sent him a piece of paper on which marks were inscribed. These sounds or marks might be some special prearranged code, or they might be "The redcoats are coming by sea." In the latter case, the sexton's verbal signaling would be indistinguishable from ordinary use of language.

If we endow a hypothetical community with a great many verbal signaling conventions for use in various activities, with verbal expressions suitably chosen *ad hoc*, we shall be able to simulate a community of language users—say, ourselves—rather well. An observer who stayed in the background watching these people use conventional verbal signals as they went about their business might take a long time to realize that they were not ordinary language users. But an observer who tried to converse with them would notice some deficiencies. He would find that every verbal expression they used was conventionally associated with some readily observable state of

[1] On this definition, a verbal expression can exist which is never uttered. See Quine, *Word and Object*, pp. 194–195.

affairs, or with some definite responsive action, or with both. And he would find that they could use only finitely many verbal expressions, so that the conventions governing their verbal signaling could be described by mentioning each expression they used.

We shall consider later how verbal signaling falls short of the full use of language. Yet it remains true that our hypothetical verbal signalers do not do anything we do not do. We just do more. Their use of language duplicates a fragment of ours.

Their use of language is covered by signaling conventions. What about ours, on those occasions when ours is just like theirs? I see no reason to deny that we too have verbal signaling conventions. What *would* be conventional signaling if it were our only use of language does not have a different character because we use language in other ways as well. Examining the definition of a verbal signaling convention, we can verify that it is satisfied by part of our use of language.

But even if some conventions governing our use of language are verbal signaling conventions, it does not follow that these would appear in a complete specification of our conventions of language. Probably they would be subsumed under more general conventions. We recall from Chapter II.5 that specializations of conventions may be conventions in their own right. A general convention of language, covering infinitely many different verbal expressions and a wide range of situations, would have consequences restricted to finite classes of expressions and narrowly specific situations. Our verbal signaling conventions could be consequences of this kind.

4. Conventional Meaning of Signals

I have been trying to demonstrate that an adequate account of signaling need not mention the meanings of signals—at least, not by name. But of course signals *do* have meanings.

Suppose $\langle Fc, Fa \rangle$ is a conventional signaling system; σ is a signal therein; s is the state of affairs mapped onto σ by Fc; r is the response onto which σ is mapped by Fa.

Then we might call σ—in general and on any particular occasion on which it is given in conformity to the convention—a *conventional signal that s* holds; and we might say that σ *conventionally means that s* holds. For σ is evidence that *s* holds, by virtue of the fact that the communicator acts according to *Fc*, hence by virtue of the convention. Or we might call σ a *conventional signal to do r*; and we might say that σ *conventionally means to do r*. For σ is a good means of getting the audience to do *r*, by virtue of the fact that the audience acts according to *Fa*, hence by virtue of the convention.

Which way should we give the meaning of σ: as a signal-that or as a signal-to? Sometimes we can properly give it both ways—for instance, in all our examples so far. But in some cases it is only proper to describe σ as a signal *that* a state of affairs holds; in such cases, let us call σ an *indicative* signal (in the signaling system in question). In other cases it is only proper to describe σ as a signal *to* do something; in such cases, let us call σ an *imperative* signal. (Let us call σ a *neutral* signal if it is equally properly called a signal-that or a signal-to.) The difference seems to lie in the character of the plans *Fc* and *Fa*. How much discretion do they allow the communicator or the audience?

A contingency plan may or may not be *discretionary*; that is, it may or may not require an agent to deliberate about which course of action would be best for himself and his partners. I suggest that if *Fa* is discretionary and *Fc* is not, then σ is indicative; if *Fc* is discretionary and *Fa* is not, then σ is imperative; if neither or both are discretionary, then σ is neutral.

Take the sexton's signal of hanging two lanterns in the belfry. (Pretend now that the signaling system was a conventional one, not confined to a single occasion.) If the signaling system is ⟨*Fc*, *Fa*⟩, with

> *Fc*: If the redcoats are observed staying home, hang no lantern in the belfry.
>
>   If the redcoats are observed setting out by land, hang one lantern in the belfry.

If the redcoats are observed setting out by sea, hang two lanterns in the belfry.

and

Fa: If no lantern is observed hanging in the belfry, go home.

If one lantern is observed hanging in the belfry, warn the countryside that the redcoats are coming by land.

If two lanterns are observed hanging in the belfry, warn the countryside that the redcoats are coming by sea.

then hanging two lanterns is a signal that the redcoats were observed setting out by sea, and it is a signal to warn the countryside that the redcoats are coming by sea. The two descriptions seem equally proper; the signal is neutral.

But if the signaling system is $\langle Fc, Fa' \rangle$, Fa' being a discretionary variant of Fa,

Fa': If no lantern is observed hanging in the belfry, do whatever seems best on the assumption that the redcoats were observed staying home.

If one lantern is observed hanging in the belfry, do whatever seems best on the assumption that the redcoats were observed setting out by land.

If two lanterns are observed hanging in the belfry, do whatever seems best on the assumption that the redcoats were observed setting out by sea.

then hanging two lanterns is properly called a signal that the redcoats were observed setting out by sea. It would be strange to call it a signal to do whatever seems best on the assumption that the redcoats were observed setting out by sea. In $\langle Fc, Fa' \rangle$, hanging two lanterns is an indicative signal.

On the other hand, if the signaling system is $\langle Fc', Fa \rangle$, Fc' being a discretionary variant of Fc,

Fc': If it seems best that Paul Revere should go home, hang no lantern in the belfry.

If it seems best that Paul Revere should warn the countryside that the redcoats are coming by land, hang one lantern in the belfry.

If it seems best that Paul Revere should warn the countryside that the redcoats are coming by sea, hang two lanterns in the belfry.

then hanging two lanterns is properly called a signal to warn the countryside that the redcoats are coming by sea. It would be strange to call it a signal that it seems best that Paul Revere should warn the countryside that the redcoats are coming by sea. In ⟨*Fc'*, *Fa*⟩, hanging two lanterns is an imperative signal.

Fa and *Fa'* are stated in terms of different, crosscutting classifications of Paul Revere's action. *Fc* and *Fc'* are stated in terms of different, crosscutting classifications of the states of affairs. So the three signaling systems above belong to different signaling problems. Each is a signaling system in its own signaling problem, since it makes Paul Revere's action depend on the state of affairs in the best way available within the given classifications.

I have ignored ⟨*Fc'*, *Fa'*⟩ because I am not sure it gives the preferred dependence in its signaling problem—it is too likely that the sexton and Paul Revere will cross each other up. If it is a signaling system, its signals are neutral.

An agent who acts according to a discretionary contingency plan must use his judgment to respond flexibly to the whole situation as he sees it, so that he can take special action to deal with unforeseen circumstances as they arise. Paul Revere, acting according to *Fa'* and observing two lanterns, might decide it was more urgent to hide the leaders than to warn the countryside. The sexton, acting according to *Fc'* and observing the redcoats setting out by sea, might discover that they were headed for the wrong place; so it would be best not to hinder them and to wait for a more important attack later. The cost of flexibility, of course, is the risk of misinformation or misjudgment.

An agent might use his judgment even if his conventional signaling system gives him a nondiscretionary contingency plan. That is, he might decide it would be for the best to violate the signaling convention in view of unforeseen circumstances; and he might be right. But if he did, his exercise of judgment would be unexpected; whereas if he were acting according to a discretionary contingency plan in conformity to a signaling convention, it would be common knowledge that he would use his judgment.

It is not at all necessary to confine ourselves to conventional signaling systems in defining meaning for signals. Consider any signaling system $\langle Fc, Fa \rangle$ for a signaling problem S, whether or not $\langle Fc, Fa \rangle$ happens to be conventionally adopted in any population. If Fa is discretionary and Fc is not, the signals of $\langle Fc, Fa \rangle$ are indicative. Consider a signal σ and the state of affairs s mapped onto σ by Fc. We can call σ a *signal in* $\langle Fc, Fa \rangle$ *that* s holds; and we can say that σ *means in* $\langle Fc, Fa \rangle$ *that* s holds. If Fc is discretionary and Fa is not, the signals of $\langle Fc, Fa \rangle$ are imperative. Consider a signal σ and the response r onto which σ is mapped by Fa. We can call σ a *signal in* $\langle Fc, Fa \rangle$ *to do* r; and we can say that σ *means in* $\langle Fc, Fa \rangle$ *to do* r. Finally, if neither or both of Fc and Fa are discretionary, the signals of $\langle Fc, Fa \rangle$ are neutral; they can equally well be called signals-that or signals-to in $\langle Fc, Fa \rangle$; and they can equally well be said to mean-that or to mean-to in $\langle Fc, Fa \rangle$. For the most part, I shall ignore neutral signals henceforth.

We would expect that by giving the meanings of indicative signals, we give their truth conditions. And so we do. Let σ be an indicative signal that s holds, in a signaling system $\langle Fc, Fa \rangle$ for signaling problem S. Then we can call σ *true* in any instance of S in which s does hold, and *false* in any instance of S in which s does not hold.

Officially, we recall, the signal σ is an action. So we are ascribing truth and falsity to actions. We did not decide whether signals were types of actions or particular actions; nor must we decide now. The action-type σ is true or false relative to any instance of S, according as the state of affairs s does or does not hold therein. There is no reason to confine ourselves to those instances of S in which σ happens to be performed. A particular action σ of that type is true or false according as the state of affairs s does or does not hold in the instance of S in which the action σ is performed. If σ is a verbal signal, we can indulge in another harmless ambiguity: we can say that the string of sounds or marks produced by the action σ in a particular instance of S is true or false, and we can say that the verbal expression uttered in the action σ is true or false relative to any instance of S. Philosophers have argued at length over the question of which entities are the proper bearers of truth and other semantic properties; I adopt an eclectic policy, letting several different kinds of entities bear semantic properties. I see no danger, provided we are prepared to convert semantic properties into semantic relations (for instance, of verbal expressions to instances of S) whenever it is appropriate to do so.

In any instance of S, by definition of a signaling problem and a signaling system, one of the signals of $\langle Fc, Fa \rangle$ is true and the rest are false. Suppose $\langle Fc, Fa \rangle$ is a conventional signaling system in some population. Then we can describe the conventional regularity in their behavior thus: in any instance of S among them, the communicator tries to give whichever signal is true in that instance, and every member of the audience responds by doing whatever seems best on the assumption that the communicator's signal is true.

But this does not seem right. How can truthfulness be a convention? What is the alternative? Systematic *un*truthfulness? Suppose we have arranged the signals of $\langle Fc, Fa \rangle$ in some sort of cyclic order. Then the members of P could get on very happily if, whenever any signal σ was true, they gave not σ but rather the signal just next to σ in the order (say, next on the right)—a false signal. This sort of systematic untruthfulness, if uniform and uniformly expected, would do just as well as systematic truthfulness. But that is because it would *be* systematic truthfulness—not in the original signaling system $\langle Fc, Fa \rangle$, but in an alternative signaling system obtained from $\langle Fc, Fa \rangle$ by permuting the signals.

There is the solution: I have been talking throughout not about truth in general, but about truth in the signaling system $\langle Fc, Fa \rangle$. I should have stated the convention thus: in any instance of S among members of P, the communicator tries to give whichever signal is true in $\langle Fc, Fa \rangle$ in that instance, and the audience responds by doing whatever seems best on the assumption that he has succeeded in so doing. What was called a convention of truthfulness is more accurately called a convention of truthfulness in $\langle Fc, Fa \rangle$.

Given this more careful statement of the convention, we no longer have any trouble finding its alternatives. The alternative to a convention of truthfulness in $\langle Fc, Fa \rangle$ would be a regularity of truthfulness in some other signaling system $\langle Fc', Fa' \rangle$. This may be any signaling system in the problem S which is sufficiently unlike $\langle Fc, Fa \rangle$ — different enough so that it is almost always impossible to conform both to the convention and to its alternative. It is enough to require that no signal of $\langle Fc, Fa \rangle$ which is a signal of $\langle Fc', Fa' \rangle$ as well can be true in both. It is more than enough to require that the two have no signals in common; indeed, that may be impossible because there may not be enough different signals available in S. If the two signaling systems have some or all of their signals in common, then, as we foresaw, systematic truthfulness in one will sometimes or always coincide with a certain kind of systematic untruthfulness in the other.

What does *not* have an alternative, and is not a convention, is this regularity: in any instance of S among members of P, the communicator tries to give whichever signal is true *under the prevailing convention* in that instance, and the audience responds by doing whatever seems best on the assumption that he has succeeded in so doing. This regularity holds whenever the members of P have any conventional signaling system for S with indicative signals, no matter what their convention may be. We can say that a signal σ is *true* in P in an instance of S if and only if there is some suitable signaling system that is conventionally adopted in P and σ is true in that signaling system in that instance of S.

An analogous treatment is available for imperative signals. Let σ be an imperative signal to do r in a signaling system $\langle Fc, Fa \rangle$ for a signaling problem S. We can call σ *true* in $\langle Fc, Fa \rangle$ in an instance of S if almost every member of the audience does do r in that instance, and *false* in $\langle Fc, Fa \rangle$ in that instance of S if not.

Why "true"? Why not "obeyed"? My use of "true" is admittedly not standard; but "obeyed" would not be quite what I mean. Is a conditional imperative, "Do so-and-so in case such-and-such," obeyed if the antecedent turns out false? Perhaps not, but I want to call it true. Is an imperative obeyed if the imperative itself is not part of the obeyer's reason for doing what he was told to do? Perhaps not, but I want to call it true. Nicholas Rescher introduces a new expression, "terminated," to play the role I assign to "true";[2] anyone unwilling to tolerate my stretching of "true" may substitute "true or terminated." But my terminology has the advantage of pointing to a certain symmetry between imperatives and indicatives: the signal either asserts or commands a certain state of affairs to hold, and is true if that state of affairs does hold.

Suppose $\langle Fc, Fa \rangle$ is a conventional signaling system in some population. Then we can describe the conventional regularity in their behavior thus: in any instance of S among them, every member of the audience tries to respond in such a way that the communicator's signal is true in $\langle Fc, Fa \rangle$ in that instance, and the communicator gives whichever signal seems best on the assumption that the audience will succeed in so doing. Once again, we can describe their convention as a convention of truthfulness in $\langle Fc, Fa \rangle$. But in the indicative case it was up to the communicator to see to it that his signal was true, by choosing the correct signal to give; whereas in the imperative case it is up to the audience to make the communicator's signal true by responding to it correctly. Once again, the alternative to a convention of truthfulness in $\langle Fc, Fa \rangle$ would be a regularity of truthfulness

[2] *The Logic of Commands* (New York: Dover, 1966), pp. 52–61.

in some other signaling system $\langle Fc', Fa' \rangle$ for the same signaling problem, $\langle Fc', Fa' \rangle$ being sufficiently unlike $\langle Fc, Fa \rangle$.

If $\langle Fc, Fa \rangle$ is any signaling system with indicative or imperative signals, we can identify $\langle Fc, Fa \rangle$ by specifying three things. (1) We must specify the set of signals of the system; that is, the set which is to be the range of Fc and the domain of Fa. (2) We must specify, for each signal of the system, whether it is indicative or imperative. (3) We must specify, for each signal of the system, the state of affairs in which it is true. We can take this state of affairs to be a certain set of possible instances of S—those in which, as we say, the state of affairs holds. In other words, we specify truth conditions for the signals of the system.

Given these three pieces of information, Fc and Fa are determined. By looking at the truth conditions of all the signals of the system, we find all the possible instances of the signaling problem to which the system applies. If the signals are specified as indicative, we reconstruct Fc by looking at the truth conditions of the signals; if the signals are identified as imperative, we reconstruct Fa by looking at the truth conditions of the signals. Given either Fc or Fa, we find the other just by looking for a discretionary contingency plan that combines with the given plan to give the preferred dependence of responses on states of affairs.

It is possible to specify $\langle Fc, Fa \rangle$ by means of a single function $\mathcal{L}$ constructed as follows. The domain of $\mathcal{L}$ is to be the set of signals of the system. Given any signal σ of the system, $\mathcal{L}$ is to assign it an *interpretation* $\langle \mu, \tau \rangle$. The component μ, called a *mood*, indicates whether σ is indicative or imperative. It does not matter just what thing μ is. Let us take it to be a code number: 0 for indicative, 1 for imperative. The component τ of an interpretation, called a *truth condition*, indicates the state of affairs in which σ is true. We can take τ to be a set of possible instances of some signaling problem: namely, those instances in which σ is true in the sense appropriate to its mood.

If $\langle Fc, Fa \rangle$ is a verbal signaling system, its signals are actions of uttering verbal expressions. Then we may make a slight change. Let the domain of £ be the set of verbal expressions uttered in signals of the system, rather than the signals themselves. We can call any verbal expression in the domain of £ a *sentence* of £. When we have made this change, it is natural to call the function £ a *language*: the language associated with ⟨*Fc, Fa*⟩. Not that every language is thus associated with a verbal signaling system. But some rudimentary languages are, and these we have now examined in some detail. It remains to be seen how these verbal signaling languages fall short of more interesting languages.

A sentence σ of a verbal signaling language £ is *true* in £ in a particular instance of the signaling problem to which £ applies if and only if that instance belongs to the truth condition assigned to σ by £; otherwise σ is false in £ in that instance of the problem. Suppose the associated signaling system is conventionally adopted in some population; then we can say they have a convention to use the language £. Their convention can be restated thus: in any instance of the signaling problem to which £ applies, one party—communicator for indicatives, audience for imperatives—tries to make sure that the communicator utters a sentence that is true in £ in that instance; the other party acts as seems best on the assumption that the first party has succeeded in so doing. This is the familiar signaling convention, now redescribed as a convention of truthfulness in £; its alternatives would be regularities of truthfulness in other verbal signaling languages which apply to the same problem as £ but which are sufficiently unlike £.

5. Meaning$_{nn}$ of Signals

H. P. Grice, in his paper "Meaning," draws our attention to the manifest difference illustrated in the following contrasting pairs.[3]

> (1A) Herod presents Salome with the head of St. John the Baptist on a charger.

[3] *Philosophical Review*, 66 (1957), pp. 377–388.

(1B) Herod says to Salome, "He's dead."

(2A) Feeling faint, a child lets its mother see how pale it is (hoping that she may draw her own conclusions and help).

(2B) A child says to its mother, "I feel faint."

(3A) I leave the china my daughter has broken lying around for my wife to see.

(3B) I say to my wife, "Our daughter has broken the china."

(4A) The bus conductor taps the pane behind the driver so that he will turn around and notice that the bus is full.

(4B) The bus conductor rings a bell three times to inform the driver that the bus is full.

(5A) A policeman stops a car by standing in its way.

(5B) A policeman stops a car by waving.

The difference we want must be a subtle one. Our A and B cases are alike in many respects. We can contrast them with these cases, for instance:

(1C) Herod leaves the head somewhere; Salome happens to see it.

(1D) Herod leaves the head where he knows Salome will see it, correctly supposing she will not realize he left it for her to see.

(1E) Herod leaves the head where he knows Salome will see it, mistakenly supposing she will not realize he left it for her to see.

In all our A and B cases, and also in (1C), (1D), and (1E), this first condition is met:

Someone does some action that produces a belief or some other response in an audience.

In all our A and B cases, and also in (1D) and (1E) but not (1C), this second condition is met:

He intends—expects and wants—to produce that response by his action.

In all our A and B cases, and also in (1E) but not (1C) or (1D), this third condition is met:

> The audience recognizes his intention to produce that response by his action.

In all our A and B cases, but not in (1C), (1D), or (1E), this fourth condition is met:

> He intends that the audience should recognize his intention to produce that response by his action.

The difference Grice has discovered between the B cases and the A cases is given by a fifth condition:

> He intends the audience's recognition of his intention to produce that response to be effective in producing that response. He does not regard it as a foregone conclusion that his action will produce the intended response, whether or not his intention is recognized.

This fifth condition holds in every B case, but not in the A cases and not in cases like (1C), (1D), and (1E).

Whenever the fifth condition holds, Grice says that the agent *means*$_{nn}$ something by his action. More concisely, someone means$_{nn}$ something by an action if and only if he intends the action "to produce some effect in an audience by means of the recognition of this intention [namely, to produce the effect]."[4] "Means$_{nn}$" is short for "means nonnaturally"—not to suggest anything supernatural, but by contrast with the so-called natural meaning of natural signs: spots that mean measles, smoke that means fire, and the like.

I would have pointed to another difference between the A and B cases. In the B cases, but not the A cases, the audience's response is produced by means of a conventional signal, given in conformity to a signaling convention. But I am in no disagreement with Grice; for meaning$_{nn}$ is a consequence of conventional signaling.

[4]"Meaning," p. 385.

Let σ be a signal of a conventional signaling system ⟨Fc, Fa⟩. Let there be a state of affairs s and a response r such that σ is Fc(s) and r is Fa(σ). Suppose I am the communicator and you are the audience in a signaling problem of the proper kind; and, having observed that s holds, I give σ in conformity to our convention. Suppose that the case is completely normal: none of the exception clauses provided in Chapter II.4 apply to it. Then I mean$_{nn}$ something by σ. I intend σ to produce your response r by means of your recognition of this intention. Proof:

The intention with which I do σ can be established by examining the practical reasoning that justifies me in doing it. I need not actually go through that reasoning to have an intention; actions done without deliberation are often done with definite intentions. So examine my justification, in one of the versions considered in section 2. It was shown in Figure 45 (repeated below).

My decision to do σ, having observed s, is premised on my expectation that I can thereby produce r and on my desire to produce r. So I do σ with the intention to produce r.

I expect you to infer s upon observing that I do σ. I expect you to recognize my desire to produce r, conditionally upon s. I expect you to recognize my expectation that I can produce r by doing σ. So I expect you to recognize my intention to produce r, when you observe that I do σ.

My expectation that I can produce r by doing σ is also premised on my expectation that you will recognize my desire to produce r, conditionally upon s, and on my expectation that you will recognize my expectation that I can produce r by doing σ. These two premises constitute both my expectation that you will recognize my intention and my reason for expecting my intention to be fulfilled. So I expect your recognition of my intention to be effective in producing your response. I do not regard it as a foregone conclusion that my action will produce r, whether or not you recognize my intention to produce r.

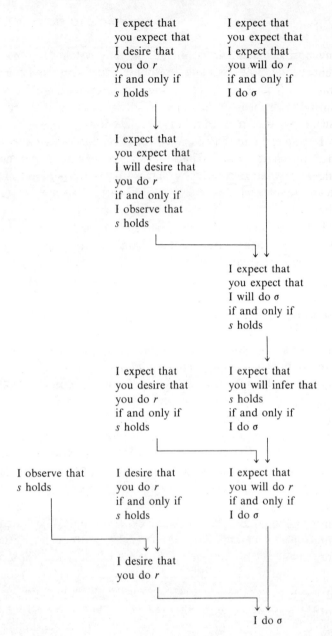

Figure 45

A conventional signal, given in normal conformity to the appropriate convention, must mean$_{nn}$ something. Is the converse true? No, for several reasons.

I might be deceiving you. My signal would mean$_{nn}$ something as usual, but I would be violating the convention.

Or I might be mistaken about the prevailing conventions and mean$_{nn}$ something by an action that I wrongly took to be a conventional signal. My reasoning, expectations, preferences, and hence intentions will look the same whether I am right or wrong. The only difference will be that I will fail to produce the intended response.

Or I might (rightly or wrongly) expect my audience to be mistaken about the prevailing conventions. That is what happens in this example from John Searle's "What Is a Speech Act?"

> Suppose that I am an American soldier in the Second World War and that I am captured by Italian troops. And suppose also that I wish to get these troops to believe that I am a German officer in order to get them to release me. What I would like to do is to tell them in German or Italian that I am a German officer. But let us suppose I don't know enough German or Italian to do that. So I, as it were, attempt to put on a show of telling them that I am a German officer by reciting those few bits of German that I know, trusting that they don't know enough German to see through my plan. Let us suppose I know only one line of German, which I remember from a poem I had to memorize in a high school German course. Therefore I, a captured American, address my Italian captors with the following sentence: "Kennst du das Land, wo die Zitronen blühen?" I intend to produce . . . the effect of believing that I am a German officer; and I intend to produce this effect by means of their recognition of my intention.[5]

It is inessential that the soldier is trying to deceive his captors. He could just as well be a real German officer who has forgotten the rest of his German from shell shock.

[5] *Philosophy in America*, ed. Max Black (Ithaca, New York: Cornell University Press, 1965), pp. 229–230.

Or I might mean$_{nn}$ something without thinking that I was conforming to a convention, and without expecting my audience to think so either. P. F. Strawson gives an example of this sort in his "Intention and Convention in Speech Acts."

> S . . . arranges convincing-looking "evidence" that p, in a place where A is bound to see it. He does this, knowing that A is watching him at work, but knowing also that A does not know that S knows that A is watching him at work. He realizes that A will not take the arranged "evidence" as genuine or natural evidence that p, but realizes, and indeed intends, that A will take his arranging of it as grounds for thinking that he, S, intends to induce in A the belief that p . . . He knows that A has general grounds for thinking that S would not wish to make him, A, think that p unless it were known to S to be the case that p; and hence that A's recognition of his (S's) intention to induce in A the belief that p will in fact seem to A a sufficient reason for believing that p. And he intends that A's recognition of his intention . . . should function in just this way.[6]

In this case an abnormality would show up if we carried S's justification of his action back one more replication. It is *not* the case that S expects that A expects that S expects that A expects that S will arrange "evidence" if he knows that p.

Or I might mean$_{nn}$ something without thinking that I was conforming to a convention, without expecting my audience to think so either, and with exactly the same sort of justification by replications as if I were conforming to a convention. Suppose I have come upon a patch of quicksand and I know of no conventional warning signal. I put a scarecrow up to its chest in the quicksand, hoping that whoever sees it will catch on. There is no convention to mark quicksand with half-submerged scarecrows; nor do I think there is or expect my audience to think so. But I do intend my action to produce awareness that this is quicksand by means of the recognition of my intention

[6] *Philosophical Review,* 73 (1964), pp. 446–447.

to produce that awareness. I have done my part of a signaling system in a signaling problem; and I hope my future audience will do its part. But if so, coordination will be achieved not by force of precedent but by force of salience.

Finally, I might mean$_{nn}$ something by an action in conformity to a convention of language, but not in conformity to any signaling convention. We have found it plausible that some use of language, but not all, is covered by verbal signaling conventions as well as by more general conventions of language. Even after we have considered what the general conventions of language might look like, I shall not try to show that any signal given in conformity to them must mean$_{nn}$ something; but I conjecture that this is true.

Searle draws this moral from his example of the soldier: "we must capture both the intentional and the conventional aspects [of communication] and especially the relationship between them."[7] I have been arguing that once we capture the conventional aspect, we are done. We have captured the intentional aspect as well.

[7] "What Is a Speech Act?" p. 230.

V | Conventions of Language

1. Possible Languages

A verbal signaling language £ has been called a language, and rightly so. But it is a rudimentary language, for at least the following reasons.

There is only a closed, finite set of sentences of £. Truth conditions can be given sentence by sentence. There is no way to create a new sentence, with its truth condition, out of old parts.

There is no such thing as idle conversation. Sentences of £ are reserved for use during some particular activity, for the sole purpose of carrying on that activity successfully. If £ is used by a convention, therefore, the convention is sustained by an interest in coordination in the short run. Anyone's failure to conform if the rest conform leads directly to an audience's response which is undesired given the state of affairs that holds.

Users of £ have little free choice. In the indicative case, a communicator who has observed a certain state of affairs and wishes to be truthful in £ must utter a certain sentence. He has no choice whether to speak or be silent; no choice what to talk about; no choice even how to phrase his message.

For any indicative sentence of £, we have stipulated that the communicator is in a position to tell whether it is true in £ on a particular occasion. There is no place for indicative sentences that express personal opinions or tentative hypotheses.

An indicative sentence is true in £ in an instance of a certain situation if a certain state of affairs holds in that instance. Indicative sentences never express general facts—only facts about the occasion of utterance of the sentence. (For the reasons listed so far, indicative sentences of £ are inadequate for carrying on speculation, deliberation, or argument.)

The audience is in a position to make true any imperative sentence of £ by a response within the situation in which it is uttered. There are no imperative sentences that convey general advice or standing orders.

The audience has an interest in making true any imperative sentence of £ uttered by a communicator who expects it to be made true. There is no need to decide whether the communicator has the knowledge and wisdom to give sound advice, or the authority to issue orders, or the power and will to enforce demands, and so on.

There are not enough moods. Though it is easy to multiply moods beyond necessity, there is no plausible way to get along with only our two. Perhaps the most urgent additional moods are: interrogative; commissive, for promises and threats; permissive, for explicit witholding of imperatives.[1] Some of these may be reducible to indicatives and imperatives, but all such reductions are problematic at best.

There is no ambiguity or indexicality in £. Each sentence has a single fixed mood and a single fixed truth condition, the same on every possible occasion of utterance within £.

Verbal signaling languages may be deficient in still more ways. But we have seen enough. Let us turn to a larger class of possible languages. I hope it will be large enough to contain languages like Welsh or English or Esperanto. If not, I hope it will at least contain large central fragments of these languages.

In this section, we shall consider what a *possible* language is, in abstraction from any users it might happen to have, and in abstraction

---

[1] See R. M. Hare, "Some Alleged Differences between Imperatives and Indicatives," *Mind,* 76 (1967), pp. 309–326, for an account of permissives as explicitly withheld imperatives. Hare suggests that we might distinguish a mood analogously related to the indicative mood: "a way of volubly and loquaciously *not* making a certain statement" (p. 321).

even from the question of how it *would* be used if it had users. Later we shall consider what it is for a population to use a language—in other words, what makes a *possible* language someone's *actual* language.

By "possible language" I simply mean an entity of the sort I am about to specify. I do not intend to say that every such entity is a serious candidate to be the actual language of any human population. There will be possible languages whose use could serve no human purpose, possible languages so clumsy that they never could be adopted, and even possible languages that men are psychologically or physiologically unable to use.

By a language, I mean an *interpreted* language. So what I call a language is what many logicians would call a language plus an interpretation for it. For me there cannot be two interpretations of the same language; but there can be two languages with the same sentences.

We shall start from the possible languages we have seen: verbal signaling languages. Such a language, we recall, is a function $\pounds$ which assigns to every verbal expression in some finite set—every sentence of $\pounds$—an interpretation consisting of a mood μ and a truth condition τ. The mood μ is a code number 0 for indicatives, 1 for imperatives. The truth condition τ is a set of possible instances of the signaling problem to which $\pounds$ applies: namely, those instances in which the sentence is true either in the indicative sense (if μ is 0) or in the imperative sense (if μ is 1). Now we must amend this description step by step for the sake of generality.

In the first place, we have seen that there should be more than two moods. Let us allow a possible language to have any finite number of moods, since we do not know an upper bound on the number that will be needed. But since there probably is an upper bound, and probably not a very high one, we will get many uninteresting so-called possible languages. That does not matter; what would matter would be to leave out interesting ones. These new moods may simply be further code numbers beyond 0 and 1: say, 2 for interrogatives, 3 for commisives, 4 for permissives, and so on, in some order for whatever others are needed. If, as we hope, some of these moods are reducible to indicatives and imperatives, we can simply leave some code numbers unused.

What difference is there between the moods, to justify us in calling them indicative, imperative, and the like? None, for the time being. As long as we abstract from the use of a possible language, moods are nothing but numbers occurring in interpretations. But later, when we see what it takes to make a possible language be an actual language of a population, different code numbers will play different roles in the conventional regularities whereby the language is used. Only then will the names we have attached to the code numbers be justified. We have already seen how this happens for a verbal signaling language: when the language is used by convention, it is the communicator who tries to make his sentences true if μ is 0, the audience that tries to make the communicator's sentences true if μ is 1.

In the second place, we can no longer take truth conditions to be sets of possible instances of the situation to which the language applies; there no longer *is* any special situation to which the language applies. Instead, we can take a truth condition to be a set of possible worlds: the set of those worlds in which, as we say, the truth condition holds. If $\mathscr{L}$ assigns an interpretation $\langle \mu, \tau \rangle$ to a sentence σ, then τ is the set of worlds in which σ is true in the sense appropriate to μ.

In the third place, $\mathscr{L}$ may contain indexical sentences whose truth conditions depend on the utterer, on his intended audience, or on the time and place of utterance. $\mathscr{L}$ may contain anaphoric sentences whose truth conditions depend on the context of previous conversation or intended subsequent conversation. (That is, sentences like "Then he took off his coat" or "The aforesaid party refused to pay.") $\mathscr{L}$ may contain sentences whose truth conditions depend on the surroundings of their utterance: "Close the door" or "There is salt on the table." So $\mathscr{L}$ must assign interpretations not to sentences themselves, but to sentences on possible occasions of their utterance. A possible occasion of utterance of a sentence σ may perhaps be identified with a pair of a possible world and a spatiotemporal location therein, such that σ is uttered at that location in that world. Given the world and location, presumably all further information we need about the context will be forthcoming. We will have uniquely identified the utterer, his intended audience, the previous conversation, the surroundings, and so on. (In those bizarre possible worlds in which more than one utterance of a sentence can occur at one location, more information about the context would have to be built into the entity we take to be the occasion of utterance. But there is no need for all occasions of utterance of sentences to be entities of the same type.)

In the fourth place, we cannot assume that sentences of £ are unambiguous. So £ must assign not an interpretation but a set of interpretations. When the sentence is unambiguous on an occasion of utterance, the set will contain just one interpretation; when the sentence is ambiguous, the set will contain finitely many interpretations. It is probably convenient to allow a third case: the set might contain *no* interpretations. That is one way to treat sentences like "The door is open" on an occasion of its utterance when no door either is present or has been mentioned; and anomalous sentences like "The kettle is dead," "Every girl sang himself a horse," or "Quadruplicity drinks procrastination" on all occasions of their utterance. (An alternative would be to treat the anomalous sentences as nonsentences, at the cost of complicating the grammar of the language; but that would not take care of "The door is open," since we do not want sentencehood itself to be relative to occasions of utterance. Another alternative would be to assign interpretations with empty truth conditions, as we would to self-contradictory sentences. That might be best; but I prefer to leave the question open.) We might like to stipulate that all the interpretations assigned to a sentence on an occasion of its utterance should have the same mood; but we should not. Consider "Shut the door" on an occasion of its utterance when a prominent open door is making everyone chilly, and when the utterer has also been telling a story and has just been asked "What did he do next?"

By now we have accumulated a large change in the character of the function £. We now have a function whose arguments are pairs of a sentence and a possible occasion of its utterance, and whose values are finite, possibly empty, sets of interpretations. An interpretation is still a pair of a mood and a truth condition; but a mood may now be any natural number (though it will be a small one if £ is an interesting language) and a truth condition is a set of possible worlds.

Originally it would have been reasonable to say that the meaning of a sentence was given by the single interpretation assigned to it by £, independently of its occasions of utterance. But we can no longer say that the meaning—or even *a* meaning—of a sentence is given by any one of its interpretations. This will not even do for a sentence that is unambiguous on every occasion of its utterance. For no indexical or anaphoric features of the sentence will show up in the interpretation it receives on any one occasion. What *does* give the meaning of the sentence—insofar as that can be done without considering the meanings of its parts—is the function whereby its set of interpretations depends on features of occasions of utterance.

Finally, we can no longer stipulate that the set of sentences of the language—the domain of £—is finite. Any interesting language has infinitely many sentences. Admittedly, at most a finite number of sentences of any language will happen actually to get uttered. At most a finite number *could* get uttered in any possible world in which human limitations remain as they are. But these finite sets are of no interest, since we have no hope of finding out which sentences they contain. It is a commonplace that any user of a language has the same competence regarding sentences that never happen to be uttered as he has regarding sentences he meets every day. Whenever this is so, his language should be taken to include all the sentences he *could* use and understand, had he enough patience, time, and memory. Unless we allow languages with infinitely many sentences, we will have to impose arbitrary and unjustifiable upper limits on the length of sentences.

2. Grammars

Not just any arbitrary infinite set of verbal expressions will do as the set of sentences of an interesting language. No language adequate to the purposes of its users can be finite; but any language usable by finite human beings must be the next best thing: finitely specifiable. It must have a finite grammar, so that all its sentences, with their interpretations, can be specified by reference to finitely many elementary constituents and finitely many operations for building larger constituents from smaller ones.

A good deal of recent effort in linguistic theory has been devoted to finding a suitable normal form for grammars.[2] The plan is to cut down the class of possible languages by cutting down the class of possible grammars, until the only possible languages left are the ones that are serious candidates for human use. In practice, this is done by restricting the normal form of grammars as far as can be done without leaving any actual language grammarless.

It will do us no harm to have many extra entities counting as possible languages, as well as the ones we really want. So we will not stipulate that our possible languages must have grammars of any specified form. In fact, we need not include possession of *any* grammar as a defining condition for possible languages. We can save ourselves the trouble of trying to say, with adequate precision and generality, what it is to have a grammar. But we must bear in mind that languages without grammars—or without grammars of whatever turns out to be the appropriate normal form—are called possible languages only because we have been too lazy to rule them out.

Let me nevertheless try to say how one sort of grammar for a possible language £ might work. I distinguish three parts of the grammar, called the lexicon, the generative component, and the representing component.

The *lexicon* is a large finite set of elementary constituents, marked to indicate their grammatical categories. Most of these will be words, or morphemes smaller than words.

The *generative component* is a finite set of *combining operations*. Each of these operates on a given number of constituents of given

[2] See, for instance, Noam Chomsky, *Aspects of the Theory of Syntax* (Cambridge, Mass.: MIT Press, 1965), chap. 1.

LEXICON

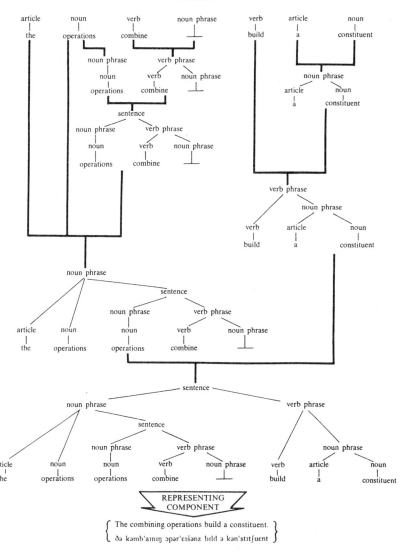

REPRESENTING COMPONENT

{ The combining operations build a constituent. }
{ ðə kəmb'aɪnɪŋ ɔpər'eɪšənz bɪld ə kən'stɪtʃuent }

Figure 46

167

categories, concatenating them to build a new, larger constituent of a given category. It also provides this new constituent with a marker showing its category and the constituents of which it is built. Starting with the lexical elements, the generative component builds up larger and larger constituents. More precisely: a constituent is any member of the smallest set containing the lexical elements and closed under the combining operations. Thus constituents are strings of lexical elements, carrying a hierarchy of category markers, as shown in Figure 46.

The *representing component* operates on some of the constituents built by the generative component—those of the category *sentence*—to produce verbal expressions. The verbal expressions thus representing sentential constituents are the sentences of £. In the special case of a *phrase-structure grammar*, the representing component has little work to do. It merely strips off the category markers and replaces the lexical items, in order, by suitable strings of sounds or marks. Grammars for formalized languages—at least, those with simple systems of punctuation—are phrase-structure grammars. In the more general case of a *transformational grammar*, the representing component does much more. Using information contained in the category markers, it may permute parts of the sentential constituent, delete parts, and add new parts, before it produces a verbal expression.

I do not stipulate that there must be a one-to-one correspondence between sentential constituents and the verbal expressions representing them. One sentence might represent several different sentential constituents: syntactic ambiguity. Or one sentential constituent might be represented by several different sentences: one kind of stylistic variation. Or a sentential constituent might fail to be represented; by permitting the representing component to be selective, we can simplify the generative component.

The grammar should give not just the sentences of £ but also their interpretations on their occasions of utterance. It can do this by (1) assigning interpretations—we shall soon consider what sort of things these are—to the lexical elements, (2) providing, for each combining operation used to build a new constituent ξ out of old ones $\xi_1 \ldots \xi_k$, an accompanying *projection operation* to derive an interpretation for ξ, given an interpretation for each of $\xi_1 \ldots \xi_k$, and (3) passing on the interpretations of sentential constituents to the sentences representing them. As the combining operations build up infinitely many larger and larger constituents, starting with the lexical elements, the corresponding projection operations work in parallel to derive interpretations for those constituents, starting with interpretations of the lexical elements.

A sentence may have more than one interpretation passed on to it; this can happen in either or both of two ways. The sentence may be syntactically ambiguous, representing—and receiving interpretations from—more than one sentential constituent. An example is Chomsky's "John was frightened by the new methods," which is ambiguous although it contains no ambiguous word. Or the sentence may be ambiguous because it represents one sentential constituent that already has several interpretations. For a lexical element may be ambiguous. When it is built into a larger constituent, the different interpretations of the lexical element will in general yield different intepretations of the larger constituent. And so on, up to an ambiguous sentential constituent, represented by an ambiguous sentence. An example is "Owen is going to the bank."

We need not assume that when a new constituent ξ is built out of old ones $\xi_1 \ldots \xi_k$, *every* possible combination of interpretations of $\xi_1 \ldots \xi_k$ yields an interpretation for ξ. If that were so, ambiguity would run wild. The projection operations may be selective, working only on input combinations of interpretations which satisfy certain restrictions. But in that case, it could happen that ξ received no interpretation at all, although it was properly built up from $\xi_1 \ldots \xi_k$, all of which did have interpretations. For no combination of interpretations of $\xi_1 \ldots \xi_k$ might be an acceptable input for the projection operation. If ξ is built in turn into another constituent, that too will normally have no interpretation; for the projection operation will not be given even one complete combination of interpretations to work on. And so on, up to sentential constituents without interpretations. If such an anomalous sentential constituent is represented by a sentence, it will have no interpretation to pass on to the sentence. That is why it is possible for sentences themselves to have no interpretations. (I do not say that any good grammar for any familiar language would yield sentences without interpretations; but, as I said earlier, it seems advisable to leave the possibility open.)

A lexical element may be indexical, receiving different interpretations on different possible occasions of its utterance. (Let us say that an occasion of utterance of a constituent is any occasion of utterance of a sentence representing a sentential constituent containing it.) This dependence on occasion is passed along through projection operations to larger and larger constituents, and finally to sentences.

My sketch of the nature of a grammar for £ has been designed to have enough generality to cover two special cases: (1) the sets of formation and valuation rules used by logicians to specify the formalized languages they study, and (2) transformational grammars for natural languages, of the form recently proposed by Chomsky, Jerrold Katz, and others.[3] There are earlier proposals by Chomsky and his associates which would have allowed grammars not fitting my description; but no convincing case has been made that this original generality is needed. In any case, it does not matter whether I have given an adequate definition of a grammar, provided I have shown roughly what one would look like.

I have subscribed to Katz's account of the way in which a grammar derives interpretations for a sentence by starting with interpretations for lexical elements, using projection operations to derive interpretations for larger and larger constituents, and finally handing over interpretations from sentential constituents to the sentences repre-

---

[3] Chomsky, *Aspects of the Theory of Syntax;* Jerrold Katz, *Philosophy of Language* (New York: Harper and Row, 1966), chap. 4. My constituents, since they carry hierarchies of category markers, are the same as Chomsky's underlying phrase markers, or subtrees thereof.

senting them. But I have not endorsed Katz's account of the nature of these interpretations; that is a separate question. Katz takes them to be expressions built out of symbols called "semantic markers" which represent "conceptual elements in the structure of a sense."[4] I find this account unsatisfactory, since it leads to a semantic theory that leaves out such central semantic notions as truth and reference.

Then what is an interpretation for a constituent? We have already decided one case. An interpretation for a sentence, and hence for a sentential constituent, is a pair of a mood and a truth condition: a code number and a set of possible worlds. The mood is something peculiar to sentences; but the truth condition suggests a general strategy for providing constituents with appropriate interpretations.

Referential semantics in the tradition of Tarski and Carnap provides constituents with extensions appropriate to their categories: truth values for sentences, denotations for names, sets for one-place predicates, sets of n-tuples for n-place predicates, and so on. Given extensions for lexical elements, appropriate extensions for larger and larger constituents are derivable by projection operations (valuation rules). Interpretations had better not be mere extensions, of course, since the extension depends both on the interpretation and on accidental facts about the actual world; for instance, constituents that ought to have different interpretations turn out to be accidentally coextensive. Nevertheless, referential semantics looks like a near miss.

A truth condition specifies truth values for a sentence; but in all possible worlds, not just in whichever world happens to be actual. We can interpret a constituent of any category on the same principle, by giving it an extension (appropriate to its category) in every possible world. The idea is Carnap's; it has recently been applied to the semantics of formalized languages with intensional operators, in work by several philosophers in the tradition of Tarski and Carnap.[5]

---

[4] Katz, *Philosophy of Language*, pp. 155-156.

[5] See Rudolf Carnap, *Meaning and Necessity*, 2nd ed. (Chicago: University of Chicago Press, 1956), pp. 181-182; Jaakko Hintikka, "Modality as Referential Multi-

For instance, an interpretation for a name should give the thing named (if any) in every possible world. It can be taken as a function from possible worlds to things therein. An interpretation for a one-place predicate should give the things of which that predicate is true in any given world; it can be taken as a function from worlds to sets of things therein (or, if nothing inhabits more than one world, perhaps just as a single set containing things from various worlds). An interpretation for an n-place predicate can be taken as a function from worlds to sets of n-tuples of things therein. It is possible to provide interpretations even for constituents that resist treatment within referential semantics confined to the actual world. An interpretation for a modal operator, for instance, might be taken as a function from possible worlds to sets of truth conditions—that is, sets of sets of possible worlds.

It is this sort of interpretation—an assignment of extension in every possible world—which, I suggest, should be attached to constituents by the grammar, in order to build up to sentence interpretations of the kind we want. (Some sort of special provision would have to be made in the grammar for attaching moods.) Obviously such interpretations—like extensions in a single world—are capable of being given relative to features of occasions of utterance; for that reason, a meaning for a constituent is not any one interpretation, but rather the

plicity," *Eripainos Ajatus,* 20 (1957), pp. 49-64; Saul Kripke, "Semantic Considerations on Modal Logic," *Acta Philosophica Fennica,* 16 (1963), pp. 83-94; David Kaplan, *Foundations of Intensional Logic* (Ann Arbor: University Microfilms, 1964); Richard Montague, "Pragmatics," *Contemporary Philosophy—La Philosophie Contemporaine,* ed. Raymond Klibansky (Florence: La Nuova Italie Editrice, 1968); Montague, "On the Nature of Certain Philosophical Entities," *The Monist,* 53 (1969); Dana Scott, "Advice on Modal Logic," presented at the Free Logic Colloquium held at the University of California at Irvine, May 1968. Montague and Scott propose a unified treatment of intension and indexicality in which extensions are assigned relative to *points of reference:* combinations of a possible world and several relevant features of context—a time, place, speaker, audience, etc. Montague classifies his work as pragmatics because of this relativity to context; it does not deal with the sort of pragmatic considerations that determine which possible language is used by a given population.

function whereby its interpretation (or its set of alternative interpretations) depends on its occasions of utterance.

3. Semantics in a Possible Language

This completes our examination of possible languages. We can define certain semantic properties of sentences relative to possible languages in general, as we did relative to verbal signaling languages. But to allow for indexicality and ambiguity, these will in general be four-place relations: between a sentence σ of $\mathfrak{L}$, the language $\mathfrak{L}$, a possible occasion o of utterance of σ, and an interpretation $\langle \mu, \tau \rangle$ assigned by $\mathfrak{L}$ to σ on o. If σ is *eternal* in $\mathfrak{L}$—assigned by $\mathfrak{L}$ the same set of interpretations on every possible occasion of its utterance—we can omit mention of the occasion o. If σ is *unambiguous* in $\mathfrak{L}$ on o—assigned a single interpretation by $\mathfrak{L}$ on o—we can omit mention of the interpretation $\langle \mu, \tau \rangle$.

σ is *indicative* in $\mathfrak{L}$ on o under $\langle \mu, \tau \rangle$ if and only if $\mathfrak{L}$ assigns to $\langle \sigma, o \rangle$ a set of interpretations containing $\langle \mu, \tau \rangle$ and μ is 0. (Likewise for the four other moods named.)

σ is *true* in $\mathfrak{L}$ on o under $\langle \mu, \tau \rangle$ if and only if $\mathfrak{L}$ assigns to $\langle \sigma, o \rangle$ a set of interpretations containing $\langle \mu, \tau \rangle$ and the truth condition τ holds in—that is, contains—the possible world w in which the possible occasion o of utterance of σ is located.

σ is *false* in $\mathfrak{L}$ on o under $\langle \mu, \tau \rangle$ if and only if $\mathfrak{L}$ assigns to $\langle \sigma, o \rangle$ a set of interpretations containing $\langle \mu, \tau \rangle$ and the truth condition τ does not hold in the possible world w in which o is located.

In speaking of the truth and falsehood of eternal sentences of $\mathfrak{L}$, either we will mention a possible world w or we will be speaking of the actual world.

σ is *true* in $\mathfrak{L}$ in world w under $\langle \mu, \tau \rangle$ if and only if $\mathfrak{L}$ assigns to σ on every possible occasion of its utterance a set of interpretations containing $\langle \mu, \tau \rangle$ and the truth condition τ holds in the possible world w. (Likewise for falsehood.)

σ is *true* in $\mathfrak{L}$ under $\langle \mu, \tau \rangle$ if and only if $\mathfrak{L}$ assigns to σ on every possible occasion of its utterance a set of interpretations containing $\langle \mu, \tau \rangle$ and the truth condition τ holds in the actual world. (Likewise for falsehood.)

In the simplest case, we can ascribe truth in $\mathfrak{L}$ to an unambiguous eternal sentence of $\mathfrak{L}$. In the absence of contrary stipulation, this is to be taken as truth in the actual world.

σ is *true* in $\mathfrak{L}$ if and only if $\mathfrak{L}$ assigns to σ on every possible occasion of its utterance a single fixed interpretation $\langle \mu, \tau \rangle$ and the truth condition τ holds in the actual world. (Likewise for falsehood.)

Truth conditions assigned by $\mathfrak{L}$ may be universal, holding in—that is, containing—every possible world; or they may be empty, holding in no possible world; or they may be in between, holding in some but not others. Accordingly, we may call sentences analytic, contradictory, or synthetic in $\mathfrak{L}$, on occasions and under interpretations.

σ is *analytic* in $\mathfrak{L}$ on o under $\langle \mu, \tau \rangle$ if and only if $\mathfrak{L}$ assigns to $\langle \sigma, o \rangle$ a set of interpretations containing $\langle \mu, \tau \rangle$ and the truth condition τ holds in every possible world.

σ is *contradictory* in $\mathfrak{L}$ on o under $\langle \mu, \tau \rangle$ if and only if $\mathfrak{L}$ assigns to $\langle \sigma, o \rangle$ a set of interpretations containing $\langle \mu, \tau \rangle$ and the truth condition τ holds in no possible world.

σ is *synthetic* in $\mathfrak{L}$ on o under $\langle \mu, \tau \rangle$ if and only if $\mathfrak{L}$ assigns to $\langle \sigma, o \rangle$ a set of interpretations containing $\langle \mu, \tau \rangle$ and the truth condition τ holds in some possible worlds but not in others.

Again, we can simplify the definienda in speaking of sentences that are eternal in $\mathfrak{L}$, unambiguous in $\mathfrak{L}$ on o, or both.

σ is *analytic* in £ if and only if £ assigns to σ on every possible occasion of its utterance a single fixed interpretation $\langle \mu, \tau \rangle$ and the truth condition τ holds in every possible world. (Likewise for contradiction and syntheticity.)

Note that an unambiguous indexical sentence may be true in £ on every possible occasion of its utterance without being analytic in £ on any occasion. Sentences reputed to have this status in English include "I am here now," "I exist," "I am awake," "I am uttering something," and the like.[6] Such a sentence, on any possible occasion of its utterance, is assigned a truth condition that holds in the world in which the occasion of utterance is located, but does not hold in some other possible world. It is reassuring to find that we have not confused this status with analyticity, as would be all too easy to do.

There is an opposite possibility that is not reassuring and comes as a surprise. An unambiguous indexical sentence may be analytic on one possible occasion of its utterance, but false on another. Take the English sentence "It is a perfect square." Take an occasion of its utterance on which the only entity under discussion in the previous conversation was the number 49, referred to by the numeral "49." Then I take it that the truth condition assigned to our sentence on that occasion will hold in every possible world in which 49 is a perfect square—that is, in every possible world. So it is the universal truth condition. The sentence is analytic in English on that occasion. But take another occasion of its utterance in which the entity under discussion was the number 48, referred to by the numeral "48." On

---

[6] All these familiar examples are subject to objections. (1) "Here," "now," and the present tense might refer, in some cases, not to the place and time of the occasion of utterance but rather to the place and time of the intended occasion of hearing. (2) A ghost who claimed to exist might do so falsely, if there is a sense in which to exist—for a human or ex-human—is to be alive. (3) A man talking in his sleep might succeed in performing the action of uttering something. I mention these objections not to uphold or attack them, but only to say that I am interested in the *status* that has been ascribed to my examples—not in whether they are really good examples of that status.

that occasion, our sentence is not analytic in English; it is false, and indeed contradictory, in English.

I find nothing wrong with this. Recall that most discussion of analyticity has ignored analytic indexical sentences; we ought to have no firm expectations about them. Moreover, although our sentence is analytic in English on certain occasions, it is not analytic in English *simpliciter*, according to the definition given; but some other indexical sentences like "Yesterday is past" are not only analytic in English on occasions of their utterance, but also analytic in English *simpliciter*. Any possible occasion of utterance of the sentence "Yesterday is past" is located on some day *d*. The truth condition assigned to the sentence on that occasion holds in every possible world in which day $d-1$ precedes day *d*; this is the universal truth condition, no matter what *d* is. So our sentence is assigned a single fixed interpretation on every possible occasion of its utterance, and this interpretation contains the universal truth condition.

Customarily, a sentence of any mood may be called contradictory; but only an indicative sentence may be called analytic. I have ignored this pointless restriction: analyticity—like contradiction, truth, and falsehood—depends on the truth condition assigned by £, without regard to the accompanying mood. An analytic imperative is, "Wear a hat or else don't!" An analytic commissive is "I promise to remain unmarried so long as I am a bachelor." An analytic permissive is "You may respire whenever you breathe." (For reasons to be considered later, I doubt that there is any such thing as an analytic question.)

This completes my quick, but highly general, account of possible languages and of the semantic properties of sentences therein. We turn now to the question: if £ is a possible language, and *P* is a population of agents, what relation must hold between £ and *P* in order to make it the case that £ is an actual language of *P*? The obvious answer is: the members of *P* must *use* the language £. But that answer is neither informative nor clear. They must use £ in a certain way. If everyone in *P* used £ by telling lies in £ or by singing operas in £ (without understanding the words), they would be using

£ but not in the right way; £ would not be their language. Only when we already know what makes a language be an actual language of a population can we say what kind of use we had in mind.

The next answer is: the members of P must give to the sentences of £ the interpretations (on occasions of utterance) which are assigned to them by £. But this is another uninformative answer. What sort of action is it to give an interpretation to a sentence? Not something anyone can do just by putting his mind to it. I can't say "It's cold here" and mean "It's warm here"[7]—at least, not without a little help from my friends.

4. Conventions of Truthfulness

We are trying to find out what the members of a population P must do in order to make it the case that a certain possible language £ is their actual language—that they *use* £, in the sense we are after. It is surely something they do in conformity to a convention: something everyone in P does because he expects his conversational partners in P to do it too, and because a common interest in communicating leads him to want to do his part if they do theirs. This much we know, just because we know that it matters little (in the long run) which language we use, so long as we all use the same one.

I shall contend that the convention of language whereby the members of a population P use a given possible language £ may best be described as a convention of truthfulness in £.[8] That is the conclusion we already reached for the special case in which £ was a verbal

---

[7]Ludwig Wittgenstein, *Philosophical Investigations* (Oxford: Blackwell, 1958), sec. 510.

[8]I owe this proposal to Erik Stenius, "Mood and Language Game," *Synthese,* 17 (1967), pp. 254–274. He proposes that language use is governed by rules giving truth conditions for sentence-radicals (sentences minus their indicators of mood) and by rules prescribing the appropriate sort of truthfulness for each mood. He considers three moods: indicatives, imperatives, and yes-no interrogatives. I have adapted his proposal by building truth conditions into the identification of possible languages and by taking his rules of truthfulness as conventions of truthfulness. Stenius in turn acknowledges a debt to Dr. H. Johansen of Copenhagen for "the idea that speaking the truth can, in a sense, be regarded as a semantic rule."

signaling language. In that case, we deduced the existence of a convention of truthfulness in £ from (1) our previous account of signaling conventions, and (2) our application of the concept of truth to conventional signaling. Now we shall consider how less restricted languages also might be used in conformity to conventions of truthfulness.

Let us postpone consideration of the nonindicative moods, of indexicality, and of ambiguity. We then have a language £ that assigns to each of its sentences a single interpretation with the indicative mood, the same on every possible occasion of utterance of that sentence. To be truthful in £ is to try not to utter any sentence of £ that is not true in £; but it is not only that. One cannot be truthful in £ just by never uttering sentences of £. (I am not now being truthful in Welsh.) To be truthful in £, in a more positive sense, is to participate in verbal exchanges by occasionally uttering sentences of £, while trying not to utter any that are not true in £. One can, of course, be silent at any particular point in a conversation without ceasing to be truthful in £; but hold your tongue too long—or at too high a cost to your social purposes—and you gradually turn from a truthful user of £ (who happens not to want to say anything) to a nonuser of £.

We did not have to distinguish between positive and negative truthfulness with respect to verbal signaling languages, because the signaling convention left no choice whether to speak or to be silent. To conform, one must utter whichever sentence of the language is true. But it would be absurd to claim that our conventions of language prohibit silence at any point in an ordinary conversation. And yet anyone who *always* chooses silence cannot be said to conform to our conventions of language.

If our simple language £ is the actual language of a population *P*, we will certainly find a regularity *R* of truthfulness in £. Members of *P* will exchange utterances of sentences of £, and they will almost always try to avoid uttering sentences not true in £. (Sometimes they will lie; but we can tolerate exceptions to a conventional regularity. Sometimes they will be mistaken; but the regularity I have in mind is that of *trying* to be truthful in £, not of succeeding. Conventions are regularities in choice of action.) Moreover, it will be common knowledge in P that members of P almost always conform to R. How about the other conditions for the conventionality of R?

Any member of P will (almost always) want to conform to R if other members of P do; they also will want him to do so; and these preferences will be common knowledge in P. We can safely assume that £ is a useful language, since otherwise it could not be the actual language of P. Then uniform truthfulness in £ permits successful communication, which answers to all sorts of interests of the members of P. Consider any ordinary conversation among members of P. Someone wants to get the others to share some of his beliefs. It does not matter why he wants them to have those beliefs—he might want them to act on those beliefs, for selfish or altruistic reasons; he might be trying to educate them; he might just be passing the time of day. He can accomplish his purpose by uttering sentences he takes to be true in £—that is, by the proper kind of conformity to R. And the reasons he can accomplish his purpose by conforming to R is that others have conformed to R in the past: namely, those who shaped the habits and expectations of his present audience. Because of the prevailing regularity of truthfulness in £, his audience has become accustomed to truthfulness in £. They are habitually truthful in £. They habitually act and form beliefs on the assumption that others are truthful in £. Being practiced in £, they do so quickly and easily. In this way, members of P normally have reason to be truthful in £, conditionally upon recent widespread truthfulness in £ by members of P.

On this account, the coordination achieved by uniform truthfulness in £ is diffuse, one-sided coordination among communicators who, at different times, communicate with the same audience. Each communicator wants to be truthful in £ because that is what past communicators have led the audience to expect. A member of the audience, as such, is not constrained by convention. He merely listens and perhaps forms beliefs, in the knowledge that the communicator is probably being truthful in £. Only when he takes his turn as communicator does he himself act in conformity to the convention of truthfulness in £.

The case of a verbal signaling language with indicative signals was described differently. The convention of truthfulness is two-sided: the communicator tries to utter a sentence true in the language, and the audience acts as seems best on the assumption that he has succeeded in doing so. The coordination sought is coordination between communicator and audience.

I think we are right to treat the two cases differently. Verbal signaling is carried out with some definite end in view, and it is common knowledge what that end is. But this is not the case in general. I do not tell you only what you need to know right now in order to serve our common purposes. Often there is nothing in particular that the audience should do if the communicator has told the truth. The audience should form a belief, perhaps, but that is normally not a voluntary action and hence not an action in conformity to convention. Even if the audience should act, the action may not answer to an interest common to the communicator and the audience, may not be one the communicator intended to produce, and so on; and hence it may not be plausibly describable as constrained by convention. No doubt there is a continuous spectrum from verbal signaling to idle chat, and two-sided and one-sided coordination may be mixed in various proportions. But generality is served by concentrating on the one-sided coordination among communicators which is present in all conventional indicative communication, not on the occasional two-sided coordination between a communicator and his audience.

Finally, a convention must have an alternative. If R is a convention of truthfulness in £, its alternatives are regularities of truthfulness in suitable alternative possible languages. For several reasons, not every other possible language is a suitable alternative. Remember that many bizarre entities are still being called possible languages because we did not go to the trouble of ruling them out. We will not be able even to define truthfulness with respect to an arbitrary possible language, but only with respect to one that confines itself to the first few moods and does not have too much ambiguity. Even so, we will have grammarless languages, trivial languages, unpronounceable languages, unlearnable languages, languages whose shortest sentences take hours to utter, languages in which no sentence says anything anyone would ever want to say, and so on. An alternative language to $\mathcal{L}$ must be a possible language for which truthfulness is definable, and one that is sufficiently convenient and useful to make it a serious candidate for human use. But it must not be too close to $\mathcal{L}$, since it must almost always be impossible to act in conformity both to a convention and to its alternative. If $\mathcal{L}$ and its alternatives shared some sentences, and assigned those sentences overlapping truth conditions, it might become possible to be truthful in $\mathcal{L}$ and in its alternative at the same time. Still we need have no fear that the convention of truthfulness in $\mathcal{L}$ will lack an alternative. There are all the actual languages of different populations, and plenty of other possible languages that would serve as well as they do.

We have now completed our survey of the defining conditions that must be met if there is to be a convention in P to be truthful in the simple language $\mathcal{L}$; and we have found that, on the supposition that $\mathcal{L}$ is the actual language of P, these conditions would be met. There would prevail in P a convention of truthfulness in $\mathcal{L}$. This convention would be sustained by a certain sort of interest on the part of members of P: an interest in communication, in being able to control one another's beliefs and actions, to some extent, by means of sounds and marks.

One is inclined to deny that there can be a convention of truthfulness in $\mathcal{L}$, on the grounds that truthfulness is a moral obligation. This objection rests in part on confusion between truthfulness in a given possible language $\mathcal{L}$ and truthfulness in the language of one's population, whichever possible language that may be. It is the former, not the latter, which is conventional. But both are obligatory, according to our common moral opinions. I am obligated to be truthful in $\mathcal{L}$, on condition that my fellows are truthful in $\mathcal{L}$; I am obligated to be truthful in whichever language they use, on condition that they do use some language or other. I grant that these are moral obligations, but I deny that they prevent truthfulness in £ from being conventional.

Why might they seem to? I suppose because conventions, as they have been defined, are sustained by preference. To conform to a convention of truthfulness in £ is to be truthful in £ because it answers to one's own preferences to do so, given that others do. But virtuous people feel bound by an obligation to be truthful in £ if others are, even if that goes against their preferences.

This much is true: one who is truthful in £ against his own preferences cannot then be acting in conformity to a convention. But such cases are exceptional. In the world as we know it—and as it must be, if use of language is to persist among sinful men—almost everyone almost always has reason to get others to share his beliefs, and therefore has reason to conform to conventions of truthfulness. Thus in the normal case, one can both be fulfilling a moral obligation and be acting according to one's preferences. Whenever that is so, we can have a case of conformity to convention. Only some exceptional cases need to be described otherwise.

A convention of truthfulness in £ is a social contract as well as a convention. Not only does each prefer truthfulness in £ by all to truthfulness in £ by all but himself. Still more does each prefer uniform truthfulness in £ to Babel, the state of nature. So each ought to recognize an obligation of fair play to reciprocate the benefits he has derived from others' truthfulness in £, by being truthful in £ himself. In the exceptional cases, this obligation will be his only reason to be truthful in £. In the normal cases, it will be present but redundant, since he will also have sufficient self-interested reasons.

A different objection can be made to my contention that conventions of language are conventions of truthfulness in a given possible language £. Recall what £ is: a certain function whose arguments are pairs of a sentence (a finite sequence of types of sounds or of marks) and a possible occasion of its utterance (a pair of a possible world and a spatiotemporal location therein) and whose values are sets of interpretations (pairs of a code number and a set of possible worlds). Now it is incredible that any ordinary user of £ has a concept of any such complicated entity. So how can he be party to any convention regarding £? How can we have expectations and preferences regarding truthfulness in £?

My answer is that he can have them *in sensu diviso*; to do that, he does not need to share our complicated concept of a possible language. He does not even need to share our concepts of function, sequence, set, pair, and possible world. He can be a nominalist philosopher who disbelieves in all of these things or a peasant who has never heard of any of them. All he has to do is to come up with the right expectations and preferences regarding particular instances of what we—but not he—would call truthfulness in £. And these particular instances are pieces of perfectly commonplace human thought and action. The only explicit use of esoteric concepts is ours, when we summarize an enormous and varied body of belief-governed action by classifying it under an invented description: truthfulness in £.

It is logically possible, then, to conform to a convention of truthfulness in £ without having any general concept of truthfulness in £. This is not to say that it is *psychologically* possible to do so without having something closely analogous to that concept; and I mean to say no such thing. The user of £ is a finite being with very limited experience; yet somehow he has acquired an enormous, and enormously varied, repertory of propensities to action, expectation, and preference in a wide variety of situations. That is what it takes for him to be—as we but not he would say—habitually truthful in £ and accustomed to expect truthfulness in £ on the part of others. I can imagine no explanation of this competence which does not posit some sort of unconscious counterpart of a general concept of truthfulness in £.

Consider a bicycle rider. Any credible theory of his competence will ascribe to him unconscious mental processes closely analogous to the use of general physical concepts, in the knowledge of general physical laws. But unless our bicycle rider happens also to be a physicist, it would be wrong to say that he had those concepts or knew those laws, although his expectations regarding a wide variety of particular situations would work according to those laws.

This completes my account of conventions of truthfulness in simple languages without nonindicative moods, indexicality, or ambiguity. Still postponing indexicality and ambiguity, let us turn to truthfulness in languages with imperatives, interrogatives, commissives, and permissives.

Recalling our discussion of imperatives in verbal signaling languages, we can think of imperative truthfulness roughly as obedience. That is, it is up to the audience to make imperative sentences of £ true in £, by trying to act in such a way that the truth conditions assigned to them by £ will hold.

As a first approximation, we might consider this statement of a convention among members of P of truthfulness in £, insofar as it applies to imperatives: if any member of P thinks he has been the intended audience of an utterance by another member of P of an imperative sentence σ of £, then he tries to make σ true in £.

This is not a very good approximation. We certainly have no convention to make true just any imperative. There are bad advice, unauthorized orders, exorbitant requests, unenforceable demands, and so on. All of these are imperatives that we can ignore without violating a convention. It is only when the communicator stands in a certain *relation of authority* to his intended audience that the audience will violate convention if they fail to try to make the communicator's imperatives true. At least in many cases, and perhaps in all, the appropriate relation of authority is as follows: the communicator and his audience have—and it is common knowledge between them that they have—a common interest in making it possible for the communicator to control the audience's actions, at least within a certain range, by uttering verbal expressions.

This relation holds between the communicator and the audience in any signaling problem with verbal signals, by our definition of a verbal signaling problem. It holds whenever the communicator is advising the audience, and it is common knowledge that he is in a position to give good advice and wants to do so. It holds whenever the communicator gives the audience an order in the course of performing some cooperative task, if it is common knowledge that this is what he is doing. It holds whenever the communicator makes a request that is not exorbitant and it is common knowledge that the audience wants to please him.

But this relation of authority does not seem to hold between a communicator and an audience when the communicator's imperative is a demand enforced by a threat. The opposite holds: it is common knowledge that the audience would be better off if the communicator were *not* able to control their actions. Perhaps an audience giving in to a demand should not be described as conforming to a convention of truthfulness, although we can concede that demanding by means of imperatives is possible because of the existence of conventions of truthfulness governing those imperatives in other situations, situations in which the communicator does stand in a relation of authority to the audience. Or perhaps we should say that demands are best analyzed not as imperatives but as commissives—threats—even when they are grammatically like imperatives.

We have arrived at the following statement of a convention of truthfulness in $\mathcal{L}$, insofar as it applies to imperatives. If a member x of P thinks he has been the intended audience of an utterance by another member y of P of an imperative sentence σ of $\mathcal{L}$, and if y and x have—and it is common knowledge between them that they have—a common interest in making it possible for y to control x's actions within a certain range by uttering verbal expressions, and if there is some action in that range whereby x could try to make σ true in $\mathcal{L}$; then x does try to make σ true in $\mathcal{L}$.

I said that a convention of truthfulness in $\mathcal{L}$ constrained the communicator of an indicative, but not the audience; likewise I am now representing the convention as constraining the audience of an imperative, but not the communicator. But in this case I see no good reason not to include the communicator: his part is to utter imperatives as seems best, assuming truthfulness in £ on the part of his audience. That is, when he stands in the relation of authority to an audience, he utters those imperatives that he wants the audience to make true in £ and that the audience can make true in £ by actions within the acceptable range of control. On the other hand, it does not seem clearly necessary to include the communicator's part in a statement of the convention. We can just as well represent him as doing what seems best, in the knowledge that the convention exists and that his audience will probably conform to it. As in the purely indicative case, we do not need to concentrate on the short-term, two-sided coordination between a communicator and his audience. There is also a long-run, diffuse coordination among all those who converse with any given person. For whoever converses with him both influences his linguistic habits and accomplishes various conversational purposes—or fails to accomplish them—by virtue of the linguistic habits he already has.

Turning to interrogatives, we can save ourselves some work. Instead of treating interrogatives as a new mood, we can treat them as a species of imperative. (Therefore the code number 2 reserved at the beginning of this chapter for the interrogative mood will not occur in interpretations assigned by the languages we are considering.) Take the question "Is dinner ready?"; compare it with the imperative "Tell me whether dinner is ready!" or, more explicitly, "Say 'yes' if dinner is ready, 'no' if not!" Or take the question "What is your name?"; compare it with the imperative "Say your name!" Or take the question "Tell me, who first reached Greenland?"; compare it with the imperative "Tell me who first reached Greenland!" I can find no important differences in any of these pairs. So I propose that questions are imperatives—imperatives with a distinctive subject matter, marked by a distinctive grammatical form. Like any imperative, a question is made true in £ by its audience's performance of the commanded action: the action we call giving a true answer to the question. A true question is a truly answered question.[9] Truthfulness in £ with respect to questions consists in trying to give true answers, at least when the questioner stands to one in a relation of authority. This is simply a special case of truthfulness in £ with respect to imperatives. At the same time, it is a special case of truthfulness in £ with respect to indicatives; the answers—at least when they are complete sentences—are indicatives, as well as being actions that make imperatives true.

I said in passing that I doubted there were analytic questions. If questions are imperatives, analytic questions are imperatives that cannot fail to be made true; for sentences of any mood are analytic in £ if and only if they are assigned the universal truth condition. So they are questions that cannot fail to be answered truly. But any question properly so-called has contrary alternative answers. Moreover, one can fail to answer truly by keeping silent and so failing to answer at all.

The commissive mood of promises and threats is akin to the indicative. It is up to the utterer to be truthful in £, by trying to see to it that the truth condition of his commissive holds. To make a promise or threat true in £ is to fullfil it, to do what one has said one was going to do. My indicative "I shall return" and my commissive "I will return" are both true in English if and only if I subsequently return; and to be truthful in English, I must try to make sure that I utter either sentence only if, later, I do return. That is, I must try to act in such a way that there is a correspondence between my words now and my deeds later. But there are two different times at which I may try to make sure of this correspondence: now, when I choose my words, or later, when I choose my deeds.

In the case of the indicative "I shall return," to be truthful is to

---

[9] Here I disagree with Stenius. He proposes, in "Mood and Language Game," that the sentence-radical of a yes-no question be considered true if and only if "yes" is the correct answer. Thus he prescribes this sort of truthfulness for questions: "Answer the question by 'yes' or 'no,' according as its sentence-radical is true or false" (p. 273). Certainly that is the most natural notion of truth for yes-no questions; but unlike mine, it cannot be extended to other kinds of questions.

try *before* I utter the sentence to make my words correspond to my deeds. I do this by trying to foresee or decide whether I will return, and by refraining from uttering "I shall return" if I foresee or decide that I will not. It is irrelevant to my truthfulness that I do or do not go on trying to make sure of the correspondence after my utterance. (It *is* relevant to whether my sentence is true; but to be truthful is to *try*—not necessarily succeeding—to make sentences true.) Rash self-prediction is untruthful; unforeseen violation of a self-prediction is not.

In the case of the commissive "I will return," to be truthful is to try *after* I utter the sentence to make my words correspond to my deeds. I do this by remembering my words and accordingly trying to return. It is irrelevant to my truthfulness—though relevant to whether my sentence is true—that I did or did not try before my utterance to make my words correspond to my deeds. Unforeseen failure to try to keep a promise is untruthful; rash promising is not.

If members of a population P are truthful in $\mathcal{L}$, and σ is an indicative sentence of $\mathcal{L}$, they will try before uttering σ to judge whether the truth condition assigned to σ by $\mathcal{L}$ holds. If σ is a commissive sentence of $\mathcal{L}$, they will try after uttering σ to act in such a way as to bring it about that the truth condition assigned to σ by $\mathcal{L}$ holds. Suppose they have a convention of truthfulness in $\mathcal{L}$. Then in doing either of these things, they are conforming to convention. They *may* do other things too: try to make indicatives true which have already been uttered, try not to utter commissives they foresee will not be made true. But these actions are not covered by the convention of truthfulness in $\mathcal{L}$. Among ourselves, they are covered by no convention at all.

A previous discomfort is apt to recur. The whole point of promising—or threatening, as strategists know—is to bind oneself to do something whether or not it turns out, at the time, to answer to one's preferences (so that others' expectations about one's action may be firmer than their expectations about one's preferences). But an action in normal conformity to convention is, by definition, an action that answers to one's preferences. So how can keeping a promise be done in conformity to any convention? It cannot—when it really does go against preference. But when preference agrees with promissory obligation, there is no reason why keeping a promise should not be done in conformity to a convention. The latter is the normal case, and it must be in any population with a convention of truthfulness in a language containing commissives. That should not surprise us: we normally keep promises because we do not want to disappoint others' legitimate expectations; because good will come of it, given what others have done in the expectation that the promise will be kept; because we do not want to incur retaliation, destroy our reputations for keeping promises, or undermine confidence in promises generally. We normally do prefer to keep our promises. And this is a conditional preference, of the kind required if promise keeping is to be action in conformity to convention. If others did not generally try to make true in £ the commissive sentences of £ which they have uttered, no one would have any of the reasons I mentioned for preferring to try to make true in £ the commissive sentences of £ that he has uttered. Any promise has the power to bind an honorable man against his preferences. But most promises are never called upon to exercise that power.

Permissive sentences are neutralizers of imperatives and commissives. If I permit someone to do something (or leave something undone), I ordinarily cancel some command I have given him or some promise he has given me. He can take advantage of my permission by acting in a way that would otherwise have been untruthful, hence contrary to our convention as it applies to my original command or his original promise. Because of my permission, his acting in that way is not untruthful. The cancellation may be complete or partial: having ordered you (or received your promise) to keep off my grass, I may later tell you that henceforth you may come on the grass whenever you like, or I may tell you that you may come on the grass just this once.

I shall not describe a new kind of truthfulness in £, truthfulness with respect to permissives. Rather, permissives will enter the statement of a convention of truthfulness in £ by way of an elaboration of my account of truthfulness with respect to imperatives and commissives. This is not to say that the permissive mood itself will be eliminated. Permissive sentences of £, with interpretations containing the code number 4, will remain. But our statement of a convention of truthfulness in £ will contain no part devoted only to permissives. Indeed, nothing new need be added to our statement of the convention. We need only make an observation about the nature of the truth conditions that may be assigned to imperatives and commissives in a language containing permissives.

The truth condition assigned by £ to a permissive sentence σ gives us the state of affairs which is permitted to hold when σ is uttered: the state of affairs in which, as we say, someone takes advantage of the permission he has been given by an utterance of σ. Thus we know what it is for an uttered permissive to be made true in £.

The simplest sort of truth condition for an imperative or a commissive is the set of just those possible worlds in which a certain person performs a certain action. We can call this a *positive* truth condition. But if an imperative or commissive is conditional—"Take an umbrella if it is cloudy!" or "I promise to help if you need me"—there is also a *negative* truth condition containing just those worlds in which the antecedent state of affairs does not occur. The more antecedents there are, the more different negative truth conditions. The whole truth condition of an imperative or commissive is the union of all its positive and negative truth conditions. In the case of an imperative or a commissive that can be neutralized by a permission, we have another kind of negative truth condition containing just those worlds in which neutralization has occurred. Thus my plan is to take any imperative or commissive that can be neutralized as if it were explicitly conditional upon—*inter alia*— the absence of any neutralizing permission.

More precisely, suppose we have an imperative or commissive whose positive truth condition concerns the action of a certain person

x. This imperative or commissive may also have a negative truth condition that can be described as follows: the set of all possible worlds in which any permissive sentence σ of $\mathcal{L}$ is uttered to x by anyone in a certain position, and σ is subsequently made true in $\mathcal{L}$ by x. (Neutralization occurs if the truth condition of σ falls at least partly outside the positive truth condition of the original imperative or commissive; otherwise we get a world lying both within our negative truth condition and within the original positive truth condition.) This negative truth condition will be included in the union of positive and negative truth conditions which is the whole truth condition of the original imperative or commissive.

We need not make any special provision for negative truth conditions of this kind, but only notice that they are possible. And if some imperatives or commissives of $\mathcal{L}$—not necessarily all—have such truth conditions, then the use of suitable permissives of $\mathcal{L}$ is already covered by a convention of truthfulness in $\mathcal{L}$ as it applies to imperatives and commissives.

One may object that there are situations in which permission is required but the requirement was not created by any previous imperative or promise. What situations these are will depend on the institutions of a particular population. We should not expect them to be covered by conventions purely of language. Perhaps they are not covered by any conventions. But we can think of these as by-products of the use of permissions as neutralizers of imperatives and commissives. We can say that the population has a rule or convention to act *as if* certain imperatives or commissives had been uttered: imperatives or commissives with truth conditions allowing for neturalization.

This is as far as we will go in examining truthfulness applied to the nonindicative moods. Doubtless there are more moods to be examined, but I have nothing to say about them and I do not believe they are very important to our understanding of language.

We can easily extend our consideration to a possible language $\mathcal{L}$ with unambiguous indexical sentences, assigned different interpretations on different possible occasions of utterance. In fact, there is a shortage of eternal nonindicatives in English, so we have already had to use indexical sentences to illustrate various points. Let us take the opportunity to recapitulate the statement of a convention of truthfulness in £, but this time providing throughout for the dependence of both moods and truth conditions upon occasions of utterance. Let P be a population in which the convention holds; let x be (almost) any member of P.

> If σ is a sentence of £ which would be indicative in £ on an occasion o of its utterance by x to an audience in P, then x tries to make sure that he utters σ on o only if σ would be true in £ on o.
>
> If σ is a sentence of £ which was imperative in £ on an occasion o of its utterance to x by a member y of P, and if y and x have—and it is common knowledge between them that they have—a common interest in making it possible for y to control x's actions within a certain range by uttering verbal expressions, and if there is some action in that range whereby x could try to make σ true in £ on o, then x tries to act in such a way that σ was true in £ on o.
>
> If σ is a sentence of £ which was commissive in £ on an occasion o of its utterance by x to an audience in P, then x tries to act in such a way that σ was true in £ on o.

As planned, questions and permissives have not been mentioned separately—questions because they are included among the imperatives, permissives because they enter into the truth conditions for some imperatives and commissives.

I have not yet said what truthfulness is with respect to ambiguous sentences of £. Perhaps we do not need to face the question. It might do to say merely that £ is an actual language of a population P only if there is a conventional regularity in P of truthfulness with respect to those sentences of £ that are unambiguous in £ on their occasions of utterance. This convention might be a consequence of a more general convention of truthfulness in £ with respect to all sentences of £, ambiguous or not; but we could give an account of the more limited convention without knowing what truthfulness in £ is with respect to ambiguous sentences.

Alternatively, we could try to describe a minimal standard of truthfulness in £ with respect to ambiguous sentences. Take a sentence σ which is assigned multiple interpretations by £ on an occasion o of its utterance. One can be minimally truthful in £ with respect to σ on o by taking any one of those interpretations and doing whatever one would have to do to be truthful in £ if that interpretation were the only one assigned to σ on o by £. A trickster is being truthful in this minimal way if, knowing that Owen is going to the shore of the river, he says, "Owen is going to the bank" during a conversation about Owen's lack of cash.

To describe a higher standard of truthfulness, we would have to mention our actual ways of resolving ambiguity in conversational practice. These depend, I suppose, on our opinions about each other's conversational purposes. For instance, we can ignore an interpretation assigned by £ to a sentence σ on an occasion o if that interpretation, but not some other one, is conversationally pointless: if it is common knowledge among the parties to the conversation on occasion o that if that were the only interpretation assigned by £ to σ on o, utterance of σ on o could in no way serve any conversational purpose of the utterer. We can ignore an interpretation of a sentence under which it is common knowledge that the sentence is blatantly false. We can ignore an interpretation of a sentence if it is common knowledge that neither the utterer nor any other party to the conversation notices that the sentence has that interpretation. There are only the crudest of our methods of resolving ambiguity. Yet I hesitate to propose that even these are part of the content of our convention of truthfulness in a language. It seems better to think of them as resulting from our exercise of common sense in the presence of a convention of language. In any case, we cannot build our methods of resolving ambiguity into a definition of truthfulness in £ until we understand better what our methods of resolving ambuity are.

Let us be content, therefore, to take truthfulness in a possible language £ as truthfulness in £ with respect to unambiguous sentences of the moods discussed, and perhaps also minimal truthfulness in £ with respect to ambiguous sentences of those moods.

So far, I have been content to claim that, as a matter of fact, language users are party to conventions of truthfulness. To test my claim, we must simply draw on our knowledge about what goes on when ordinary people use a language in an ordinary way. We can imagine what it would be like for a possible language £ to be an actual language of a population P more or less like ourselves, in circumstances more or less like ours. When we imagine this, I maintain, we find that on my definitions there prevails in P a convention to be truthful in £—a convention sustained by an interest of the members of P in communication, in being able to control one another's beliefs and actions to an extent by producing sounds and marks. We considered this claim first for verbal signaling languages; next for languages simplified by removal of nonindicatives, indexicality, and ambiguity; and finally for languages with these complications restored.

If it is true that conventions of truthfulness are a feature of normal language use as we know it, and if—as I suppose—they are an important feature thereof, then it might be reasonable to appeal to them in defining what it is for a possible language £ to be an actual language of a population P. That is, we might adopt the definition:

> £ is an *actual language* of P if and only if there prevails in P a convention of truthfulness in £, sustained by an interest in communication.

According to our previous discussion of verbal signaling, this definition would be adequate in the special case of verbal signaling languages; I conjecture that it is also adequate in general. That is, I conjecture that it agrees with ordinary usage in clear cases, and draws a convenient line among unclear cases. The test of the definition would be to see if we can think of clear cases in which it disagrees with our inclinations to affirm or deny that £ is an actual language of P; and I have not been able to think of any.

It is possible to argue by counterexamples that the definition does not give a necessary condition for $\mathfrak{L}$ to be an actual language of P. We can invent many bizarre cases in which we have some inclination to say that $\mathfrak{L}$ is an actual language of P although there is no convention in P of truthfulness in $\mathfrak{L}$. We can imagine a population of inveterate liars, or of people who suspect each other of being inveterate liars, or of people who use their language only to tell tall tales, or of creatures of instinct who are unable to use any language other than the one that is built into them. But none of these bizarre counterexamples is convincing, for once we appreciate how peculiar they are—how different from language use as we know it—we will not want to classify them as *clear* cases under ordinary usage. And if they are unclear cases, we are free to settle them in whatever way we find convenient. We can happily admit, of course, that they are cases in which a language is, in an extended sense, an actual language of a population; this is simply to say that they bear important resemblances to cases in which the condition given in the definition is satisfied.

5. Semantics in a Population

To the extent that we have given adequate necessary and sufficient conditions for a language to be an actual language of a population, we are in a position to define some semantic relations of verbal expressions to populations of language users. These will depend in the obvious way on the corresponding semantic relations of verbal expressions to possible languages, by way of the relation we have been examining between languages and populations. In general, we will again have four-place relations: this time, among a verbal expression σ, a population P, a possible occasion o of utterance of σ, and an interpretation $\langle \mu, \tau \rangle$.

> σ *receives* from P on o the interpretation $\langle \mu, \tau \rangle$ if and only if there exists a possible language $\mathfrak{L}$ such that $\mathfrak{L}$ is an actual language of the population P, and such that $\mathfrak{L}$ assigns to $\langle \sigma, o \rangle$ a set of interpretations containing $\langle \mu, \tau \rangle$.

If σ is *eternal* in *P*—receives the same set of interpretations from *P* on every possible occasion of its utterance—we can omit mention of the occasion *o*. If σ is *unambiguous* in *P* on *o*—receives a single interpretation from *P* on *o*—we can omit mention of the interpretation ⟨μ, τ⟩.

> σ is *indicative* in *P* on *o* under ⟨μ, τ⟩ if and only if there exists a possible language £ such that £ is an actual language of the population *P*, and such that £ assigns to ⟨σ, *o*⟩ a set of interpretations containing ⟨μ, τ⟩, and μ is 0. (Likewise for the other named moods.)
>
> σ is *true* in *P* on *o* under ⟨μ, τ⟩ if and only if there exists a possible language £ such that £ is an actual language of the population *P*, and such that £ assigns to ⟨σ, *o*⟩ a set of interpretations containing ⟨μ, τ⟩, and the truth condition τ holds in—contains—the possible world *w* in which the possible occasion *o* of utterance of σ is located. (Likewise for falsehood.)
>
> σ is *analytic* in *P* on *o* under ⟨μ, τ⟩ if and only if there exists a possible language £ such that £ is an actual language of the population *P*, and such that £ assigns to ⟨σ, *o*⟩ a set of interpretations containing ⟨μ, τ⟩, and the truth condition τ holds in every possible world. (Likewise for contradiction and syntheticity.)

Simplifying for the case in which σ is both eternal and unambiguous in *P*, we get definitions like these:

> σ is *true* in *P* in world *w* if and only if there exists a possible language £ such that £ is an actual language of the population *P*, and such that £ assigns to σ on every possible occasion of its utterance a single fixed interpretation ⟨μ, τ⟩ whose truth condition τ holds in the possible world *w*.
>
> σ is *true* in *P* if and only if there exists a possible language £ such that £ is an actual language of the population *P*, and such that £ assigns to σ on every possible occasion of its utterance

a single fixed interpretation $\langle \mu, \tau \rangle$ whose truth condition τ holds in the actual world.

σ is *analytic* in P if and only if there exists a possible language $\mathcal{L}$ such that $\mathcal{L}$ is an actual language of the population P, and such that $\mathcal{L}$ assigns to σ on every possible occasion of its utterance a single fixed interpretation $\langle \mu, \tau \rangle$ whose truth condition τ holds in every possible world.

We can simplify the definienda in a different way, retaining mention of the occasion o of utterance of σ, but not mentioning the population P. For by examining o we can identify a communicator and his intended audience, and look for an actual language of a population to which they belong. Thus we get semantic relations between a verbal expression σ and an occasion o of its utterance (and, if we need to provide for ambiguity, also an interpretation). Neither a population nor a language need be mentioned. I will illustrate the simplified definienda without provision for ambiguity.

σ is *true* on o if and only if there exist a possible language $\mathcal{L}$ and a population P such that the communicator and intended audience on o belong to P, $\mathcal{L}$ is an actual language of P, and $\mathcal{L}$ assigns to $\langle \sigma, o \rangle$ a single interpretation $\langle \mu, \tau \rangle$ whose truth condition τ holds in the possible world w in which o is located.

σ is *analytic* on o if and only if there exist a possible language $\mathcal{L}$ and a population P such that the communicator and intended audience on o belong to P, $\mathcal{L}$ is an actual language of P, and $\mathcal{L}$ assigns to $\langle \sigma, o \rangle$ a single interpretation $\langle \mu, \tau \rangle$ whose truth condition τ holds in every possible world.

So much for the interpretations given by a population to those verbal expressions that are the sentences of its language. How about the nonsentential constituents in a grammar for that language? These too carry interpretations. (Let us overlook indexicality, ambiguity, and anomaly, and pretend that they carry single fixed interpretations.)

The grammar assigns interpretations to all its constituents, either directly or by means of its projection operations. But we should like to say that a word, for instance, is given an interpretation by a population of language users. Welshmen give the word "gwyn" a certain interpretation—perhaps it is the function that assigns to every possible world the set of white things therein. In saying this, we have mentioned neither a language nor a grammar. We want a three-place relation: the constituent ξ receives from the population P the interpretation ι.

How can we define this relation? Presumably by mentioning a language $\mathfrak{L}$ and a grammar Γ to link the population P with the assigment of ι to ξ. Γ assigns ι to ξ; $\mathfrak{L}$ is given by Γ; and P has a convention of truthfulness in $\mathfrak{L}$. Unfortunately, $\mathfrak{L}$ will not have just one grammar. Different grammars for $\mathfrak{L}$ will interpret constituents differently; one of them may assign ι to ξ, another may not. Different grammars for $\mathfrak{L}$ may even analyze sentences differently into constituents; ξ may be a constituent in one grammar for $\mathfrak{L}$, but not in another. These differences between grammars for $\mathfrak{L}$ cancel out; the different grammars give the same sentences, with the same interpretations. Given P, we select $\mathfrak{L}$ by looking for a convention of truthfulness; but given $\mathfrak{L}$, how can we select Γ? Conventions of truthfulness pertain to whole sentences and leave the interpretations of parts of sentences undetermined. Perhaps we should look for conventions of some other kind, but I cannot think what the content of such a convention might be. It could not simply be a convention to adopt such-and-such grammar or a convention to bestow such-and-such interpretations upon such-and-such constituents. Conventions are regularities in action, and there is no such action as adopting a grammar or bestowing an interpretation (or if there is, it does not occur in normal use of language).

Some grammars for $\mathfrak{L}$ are simple, natural, reasonable, easy, good; others are complicated, artificial, contrived, difficult, bad. Perhaps Γ should be the *best* grammar for $\mathfrak{L}$, according to some appropriate method of evaluating alternative grammars. We can define a four-place relation among a constituent ξ, a population P, an interpretation ι, and a method of evaluation M:

> ξ *receives* from P the interpretation ι (according to M) if and only if there exist a possible language $\mathfrak{L}$ and a grammar Γ for $\mathfrak{L}$, such that $\mathfrak{L}$ is an actual language of the population P, and such that ξ is a constituent in Γ and Γ assigns ι to ξ, and such that Γ is the best grammar for $\mathfrak{L}$ according to the method of evaluation M.

If we can find a method of evaluation that uniquely deserves a privileged status, we can remove the undesired relativity to M. If not, I fear that the notion we want is indefensible: there is no such thing as *the* interpretation given to ξ by P, but only the various interpretations given to ξ by P according to the various alternative methods of evaluating grammars.

Why might some one method of evaluating grammars deserve a privileged status? Perhaps because it is the one that, as Chomsky has conjectured, enters into the psychological explanation of linguistic competence.[10] Suppose that whenever anyone acquires the ability and propensity to be truthful and expect truthfulness in a language, he does so by forming some sort of unconscious internal representation of a grammar for that language; and suppose that at any stage in a child's acquisition of language, his internally represented grammar is the *best* grammar, according to a certain fixed method M of evaluation, that fits the use of language he has observed around him. Thus it is M, together with observation, that determine which grammar a child will internally represent; and the grammar internally represented by native speakers of a language $\mathfrak{L}$ will be the grammar of $\mathfrak{L}$ that is best according to M.

This psycholinguistic hypothesis is still speculative. I can only say that if it, or something like it, is true, then there is a clear sense in which a constituent can be said to receive an interpretation from a population. If not, we must look elsewhere for a privileged method

[10] *Aspects of the Theory of Syntax,* chap. 1.

of evaluation, or we must give up. To give up would be to accept Quine's thesis of the inscrutability of reference: no matter how much we know about the population P, we have no objectively determinate way of interpreting parts of their discourse shorter than sentences.[11]

I hope we now understand what it would be for a verbal expression σ to be analytic in a population P. It remains open whether any verbal expression ever *is* analytic in any population. Analyticity as described so far might be a perfectly intelligible status which happens not to be occupied. Similarly, we may know what it would be for a possible language £ to be the actual language of a population; but we do not know that this ever occurs. And I strongly suspect that it does not.

It is often said that analyticity is not sharp. (To say this is quite different from saying that analyticity, sharp or unsharp, is unintelligible.) In any population, say ourselves, most sentences are clearly synthetic, a few trifling ones are pretty clearly analytic, and everything interesting in philosophy and the sciences seems to be somewhere in between. For instance, there seems to be analyticity somewhere in the fundamental principles of dynamics. But where? Conservation of momentum? Action equals reaction? Force equals mass times acceleration? Somewhere else? We cannot tell. Each seems, somehow, partially analytic. But how is partial analyticity possible?

Not primarily because our conventions of language are conventions to less than the highest degree, although they are. It does not seem as if a higher degree of conventionality—fewer cases of untruthfulness, firmer confidence in the truthfulness of others, fewer exceptions of various kinds—would be likely to make analyticity any sharper. And not primarily because it is unclear exactly what possible worlds there are, although it is unclear. (For instance, I have no idea whether any possible world is five-dimensional.) Since analyticity is truth—in the language of a population—in every possible world, uncertainty about the possibility of worlds could certainly be reflected in

[11] *Word and Object*, pp. 68–79; "Ontological Relativity: The Dewey Lectures 1968," *Journal of Philosophy*, 65 (1968), pp. 185–198.

uncertainty about the analyticity of sentences. But that cannot be the whole explanation of unsharp analyticity. Sometimes we cannot tell whether a sentence is analytic—say, one of the principles of dynamics—because we cannot tell whether it is true in our language in some hypothetical world that clearly *is* possible.

I think we should conclude that a convention of truthfulness in a single possible language is a limiting case—never reached—of something else: a convention of truthfulness in whichever language we choose of a tight cluster of very similar possible languages. The languages of the cluster have exactly the same sentences and give them corresponding sets of interpretations; but sometimes there are slight differences in corresponding truth conditions. These differences rarely affect worlds close enough to the actual world to be compatible with most of our ordinary beliefs. But as we go to more and more bizarre possible worlds, more and more of our sentences come out true in some languages of our cluster and false in others. So a sentence could be analytic in some languages of our cluster but false (in sufficiently remote worlds) in others. That sentence would be *partially* or *unsharply* analytic among us. Our actual language is like a resonance hybrid of the possible languages that make it up. Analyticity is sharp in any one of them, but they may not agree.

Even if it did not explain the fact of unsharp analyticity, the hypothesis that our conventions of language restrict us to clusters, not to single possible languages, would be plausible on other grounds. The sort of convention I have in mind is this: almost everyone, almost always, is truthful in at least *some* languages of the cluster: but not necessarily the same ones for everyone, or for one person at different times. This is a better convention for us to have than a convention of truthfulness in a single language. Standardization for the sake of communication is a good thing, but not all-important. If the cluster is tight enough, there is not much threat to communication. Usually we are not talking about remote worlds where truth conditions diverge; so usually truthfulness in any language of the cluster is truthfulness in every language of the cluster. When a confusing divergence does turn up, communication can be preserved—assuming a little good will—by looking for sentences whose truth conditions do not diverge in a troublesome way, and by making temporary conventions more restrictive than our permanent convention. In return for tolerating some threat to communication, we get two benefits.

For one thing, the different languages of the cluster may have different virtues and vices, and hence may be differently suited to individual opinions, tastes, and conversational purposes. If everyone can pick from the cluster, incompatible preferences among languages may all be satisfied. Moreover, by not commiting ourselves to a single language, we avoid the risk of committing ourselves to a single language that will turn out to be inconvenient in the light of new discoveries and theories; we allow ourselves some flexibility without change of convention.

But, more important, the less restrictive our permanent convention is, the less experience it takes to identify it, catch on, and begin to be party to it. A child has to extrapolate from a limited sample of language use, some of it even violating convention. Suppose everyone around him were truthful in exactly the same possible language all the time. The child might still have to wait a long time before he had observed enough conversation to allow him to identify the language. For if two languages differ only in the truth values of sentences in remote possible worlds, the difference will show up in very few conversations. Admittedly, the child is helped by his propensity to ignore almost all the extrapolations consistent with his data— otherwise he could not get anywhere. But provided that more than one language in the cluster is a serious candidate—and this I take to be proved by the existence of unsharp analyticity—he needs more information to identify a language in the cluster than to identify the cluster. So I suggest that a convention of truthfulness in a single possible language could not sustain itself. It would be imperfectly learned; having been imperfectly learned, it would frequently be violated; being frequently violated, it would be still more imperfectly learned.

Conclusion

In the introduction, I undertook to uphold the platitude that there are conventions of language. This I have now done—I do not know how convincingly. First, and at length, I have tried to say in general what a convention is; then, in a sketchy way, I have tried to say what sort of conventions might be a population's conventions of language. Thus I have tried to answer Quine's and White's skeptical challenge.

But their skepticism about conventions of language is only part of a larger skepticism: skepticism about analyticity, contradiction, syntheticity, entailment, synonymy (in the sense of mutual entailment), and the rest. As everyone knows by now, these notions are interdefinable in simple ways. If any member of the circle makes sense, every member makes sense. I have tried to make sense of analyticity. Or, rather, I have tried to make sense of two different analyticities. In Chapter V.3 I defined analyticity in a possible language $\mathcal{L}$; in Chapter V.5 I defined analyticity in a population P of language users. The latter analyticity depended on the former analyticity and on the conventional relation between a possible language and a population. If I have succeeded in rescuing the platitude that language is conventional, have I thereby succeeded in rescuing analyticity and its kin? I believe I have.

There are two kinds of semantic theory, sometimes wrongly thought to be competing efforts to do the same job: that of analyzing semantic properties such as truth, analyticity, and the rest. There is no such job to do, because there are no such properties. Instead there are pairs of semantic *relations*: truth in a language $\mathcal{L}$, truth in a population P; analyticity in $\mathcal{L}$, analyticity in P; and so on.

203

One kind of semantics analyzes truth, analyticity, and the rest in relation to possible interpreted languages, in abstraction from any users thereof. This is the kind of semantics done by Frege, Tarski, and (most of the time) Carnap. This kind of semantics used to suffer from an inability to distinguish among coextensive expressions with different senses, and from an inability to handle indexical features of language; but these deficiencies are being overcome in recent work using the idea that extensions should be assigned relative to a possible world and relative to a time of utterance, a speaker, and so on.

The other kind of semantics analyzes truth, analyticity, and the rest, in relation to an agent or a population of agents. This is the kind of semantics done by the later Wittgenstein, Grice, Skinner, Quine, Morris, Ziff, and (sometimes) Carnap. This kind of semantics often tends to suffer from an unwillingness to consider more than one verbal expression at a time.

It is a red herring to say that the first kind of semantics deals with artificial languages, whereas the second kind deals with natural languages. Both kinds have dealt with both; both kinds have worked better on simplified fragments of natural languages than on complete natural languages, just as we would expect. The builders'-assistant language game is about as much like a natural language as a first-order calculus is.

Now let us turn to part of Quine's criticism of analyticity. Quine is complaining that the accounts of analyticity given by Carnap and his associates are unhelpful. He considers the proposal that a statement is analytic in $\mathcal{L}$ if and only if it is true by virtue of the semantical rules for $\mathcal{L}$ (and by virtue of these alone); and that the language $\mathcal{L}$— at least if it is an artificial language—is an ordered pair of which the second component is a set of semantical rules specifying truth conditions. Quine replies as follows:

> But, by the same token and more simply, we might construe
> an artificial language L outright as an ordered pair whose second

component is the class of its analytic statements; then the analytic statements of L become specifiable simply as the statements in the second component of L. Or better still, we might just stop tugging at our bootstraps altogether.

Appeal to hypothetical languages of an artificially simple kind could conceivably be useful in clarifying analyticity, if the mental or behavioral or cultural factors relevant to analyticity—whatever they may be—were somehow sketched into the simplified model. But a model which takes analyticity merely as an irreducible character is unlikely to throw light on the problem of explicating analyticity.[1]

What is going on? Never mind the fact that Quine's Carnapian opponent is supposed to be talking about artificially simplified languages. Let us put into his mouth the bolder proposal that *any* possible language can be represented by an ordered pair whose second component is a set of semantical rules of truth. (What is special about an artificial language is simply that a philosopher might hope to exhibit those rules without working too hard.) That is not quite the representation we chose for our possible languages, but it is close enough. This is tugging at bootstraps, Quine says; what would not be tugging at bootstraps would be to mention mental or behavioral or cultural factors.

Quine wants to know about analyticity in *the* language *of* a given population.[2] Otherwise he has no business admitting that any information about the population could be relevant. He is perfectly right to deny that his question has been answered; for his opponent is telling him about analyticity in a possible language, without regard to any population's use of that language. Perhaps the opponent

[1] "Two Dogmas of Empiricism," pp. 35–36.
[2] This is consistent with "Two Dogmas of Empiricism," p. 33: "A statement S is said to be *analytic for* a language L, and the problem is to make sense of this relation generally, that is, for variable 'S' and 'L'." For the passage can and must be read as saying that the problem is to make sense of analyticity for an arbitrary *actual* language, identified not by its semantic properties but by its users.

supposed that Quine knew what it meant for a possible language to be the language of a population. And Quine did, in a sense: Quine knows what it means for the language of Welshmen to be the language of Welshmen. But what Quine did *not* know—and what his Carnapian opponent did not tell him[3] —was the relation that must hold between Welshmen and a certain ordered pair (whose second component is a set of semantical rules) to make that ordered pair *be* the language of Welshmen. To tell Quine that, the opponent will certainly have to mention mental or behavioral or cultural factors among Welshmen.

It seems strange that Quine has not been skeptical about truth itself. He takes it that the work of Tarski has left truth clear. But what Tarski left clear was truth in a given possible interpreted language, not truth in the language of a population. Granted that "Gwyn yw eira" is true in a certain possible interpreted language if and only if snow is white; here is Morgan saying "Gwyn yw eira"—is he telling the truth? The fact that the possible language in question is called Welsh because it is the language of Welshmen does not explain what we mean when we say that Morgan is telling the truth in his language, or what we mean when we simply say that Morgan is telling the truth. To explain that, we will have to talk about some mental and behavioral and cultural factors.

I first did more or less what Quine's Carnapian opponent was doing: I gave an account of the nature of any possible language, in such a way that it would be easy to identify the analytic sentences of a given possible language. But then I tried to finish the job by doing what Quine's opponent left undone. I gave an account of the mental and behavioral and cultural factors in a population that determine the analytic sentences of their language by determining

[3] The real Carnap does have something to say, in "Meaning and Synonymy in Natural Languages," *Philosophical Studies*, 6 (1955), pp. 33–47. The hypothesis that a given possible language £ is Karl's actual language has testable consequences regarding Karl's likely answers to "What would you say if . . . ?" questions. The trouble is that to derive these consequences from the hypothesis, we must first understand it—that is, we must know what it is for £ to be Karl's actual language.

which possible language is theirs. So I claim I have filled Quine's order: I have given an account of the proper kind of analyticity—analyticity relative to a population of language users.

Yet my answer to Quine falls short of some philosophers' hopes. I have spoken freely throughout of possible worlds, and I do not see how I could have done away with them. Isn't this the old circle at last? For every known way to explain away possible worlds turns out to appeal to analyticity. Possible worlds are models, or indices of models, or diagrams of models (state descriptions), or theories of models (complete novels) for some sufficiently rich language.[4] But of course not *all* the models for the language—only those that satisfy its analytic truths!

Even this outcome is more of a spiral than a circle. If at first we only knew what analyticity was in one special language, we could take our possible worlds as models, or whatever, for that language, and go on to use these possible worlds to explain analyticity in an arbitrary language. That would be something of an advance.

But I would rather say that the whole idea of explaining away possibility in favor of analyticity was a bad idea. Why should it be human conventions that create and destroy facts about what is possible? All that human convention can do is to select one verbal expression rather than another to enjoy the privilege of truth by virtue of the facts about the possiblity of worlds. In just the same way, human convention selects one verbal expression rather than another to enjoy the privilege of truth by virtue of the facts about tomorrow's weather. Say, if you like, that it is by convention that there are no *rightly so-called* married bachelors. But do not say that it is by convention that there are no married bachelors, in this world or any other. There couldn't be.

[4]For instance, possible worlds are explained as models in Richard Montague, "Logical Necessity, Physical Necessity, Ethics, and Quantifiers," *Inquiry,* 3 (1960), pp. 259–269; as indices of models in Kripke, "Semantical Considerations on Modal Logic;" as state descriptions in Carnap, "Modalities and Quantification," *Journal of Symbolic Logic,* 11 (1946), pp. 33–64; and as complete novels in Jeffrey, *Logic of Decision,* pp. 196–197.

In any case, by what right do we call possible worlds and their inhabitants disreputable entities, unfit for philosophical service unless they can beg redemption from philosophy of language? I know of no accusation against possibles that cannot be made with equal justice against sets. Yet few philosophical consciences scruple at set theory. Sets and possibles alike make for a crowded ontology. Sets and possibles alike raise questions we have no way to answer. Are there any uncountable sets smaller than the continuum? Are there any five-dimensional possible worlds? I propose to be equally undisturbed by these equally mysterious mysteries.

One accusation against possibles is not duplicated against sets; but possibles are not guilty as charged. Possibles are said to resist individuation. When have we one possible in two worlds, and when have we two similar possibles in two worlds? A drastic theory settles the question easily: nothing is *ever* in more than one possible world. This extreme solution shows that the difficulty is not serious; perhaps less drastic solutions would be even better.[5]

Possibles are tolerably well behaved; therefore the question whether to countenance them in our metaphysical theorizing depends on what they are good for. I believe that any fair-minded effort to make use of them in systematic ontology will show that they are good for a great deal.

Analyticity is truth in all possible worlds. What is analytic for someone depends jointly on the facts about the possible worlds and on the language he is using. The language he is using depends on the conventions he is party to. And these conventions are regularities in behavior, sustained by an interest in coordination and an expectation that others will do their part.

[5] See Lewis, "Counterpart Theory and Quantified Modal Logic."

Index